A Sacred Look:
Becoming Cultural Mystics

A Sacred Look: Becoming Cultural Mystics

Theology of Popular Culture

Nancy Usselmann, FSP

FOREWORD BY
Craig Detweiler

CASCADE *Books* • Eugene, Oregon

A SACRED LOOK: BECOMING CULTURAL MYSTICS
Theology of Popular Culture

Cascade Books
An Imprint of Wipf and Stock Publishers
199 W. 8th Ave., Suite 3
Eugene, OR 97401

www.wipfandstock.com

PAPERBACK ISBN: 978-1-5326-3571-7
HARDCOVER ISBN: 978-1-5326-3573-1
EBOOK ISBN: 978-1-5326-3572-4

Cataloguing-in-Publication data:

Names: Usselmann, Nancy. | Detweiler, Craig, foreword.

Title: A Sacred Look: Becoming Cultural Mystics : Theology of Popular
Culture / Nancy Usselmann. Foreword by Craig Detweiler.

Description: Eugene, OR: Cascade Books, 2018 | Includes bibliographi-
cal references and index.

Identifiers: ISBN 978-1-5326-3571-7 (paperback) | ISBN 978-1-5326-
3573-1 (hardcover) | ISBN 978-1-5326-3572-4 (ebook)

Subjects: LCSH: Christianity and culture. | Religion and culture. | Popu-
lar culture—Religious aspects—Christianity.

Classification: LCC BR115.C8 U7 2018 (print) | LCC BR115.C8 (ebook)

Nihil Obstat: Fr. Gustavo Castillo, S.T.D., censor ad hoc
Imprimatur: Most Reverend José H.Gomez, Archbishop of Los Angeles
           October 23, 2017

Manufactured in the U.S.A.   04/17/18

For my parents, Gregory and Anna Maria
Usselmann, who are my first teachers in the faith
and impart to me a deep love for God and our
culture through their love of beauty.

For Blessed James Alberione, Founder of
the Pauline Family, for inspiring the Church
to be at the forefront of evangelization in
a media culture.

Contents

Part 3: Theology of Pop Music

Part 4: Needs of Humanity

Foreword

Into the Mystic

O UR SENSES ARE SO inundated with information that we may be tempted to turn off all electronic inputs. We may need to close our laptops, turn off the television, and power down our smart phones to sharpen our vision. But could we also open our eyes, attune our ears, and quicken our spirits to a new way of being? The Irish singer/poet Van Morrison described how sailors exalt as they "Smell the sea and feel the sky." Morrison invites his listeners to "Let your soul and spirit fly into the mystic."[1] Sr. Nancy Usselmann is singing a similar song. She dares us to become cultural mystics, not via retreat but through active listening and perceiving. We are challenged to take a sacred look at movies and TV, to tune our ears to the Top 40 in search of transformative spiritual experiences.

There is a time-honored, church-approved tradition of cultural mystics. In Dante's *Paradiso*, his beatific vision of Beatrice inspires a meditation upon love as a cosmic principle like gravity, "The Love that moves the sun and the other stars." Clare of Assisi was named the patron saint of television because even in the thirteenth century she had visions projected on her wall when

---

1. Van Morrison, "Into the Mystic," from *Moondance*, Warner Brothers Records, 1970.

she was too ill to attend Mass. For saints like Clare, seeing and believing are intertwined. Oscar-winning director Martin Scorsese credits the book *The Six O'Clock Saints* with planting visions in his head. His frail and fallen characters like boxer Jake LaMotta are ringed by light around their heads because a boyish Scorsese was transfixed by the images of saints. Scorsese inspired screenwriter Frank Cottrell Boyce to research the lives of saints and craft the beautiful Christmas film, *Millions* (2004). The young boy at the center of the charming Scottish bank robbery story is flooded with mystical visions of lively saints. Boyce remembers seeing Jennifer Jones starring in the Oscar winning biopic, *The Song of Bernadette* (1943). He reflects, "There is something innately cinematic about Bernadette's experience: being transfixed by the image of an impossibly beautiful woman projected into a dark corner on an out-of-town development. You could say that, in a way, the early medieval saints were a prototype of the cinema."[2] Boyce suggests that, "The thing about saints is that for nearly 2,000 years they were the popular culture."[3] Perhaps Sister Nancy's bold book is pointing out something that has been evident for far longer than we realized.

Readers may be tempted to dismiss any attempt to mine spiritual truth from a violent television series like *The Sopranos*. But give Sister Nancy your time and attention as she guides us into how to recognize the good, the true, and the beautiful even amidst a seemingly fallen medium. She invites us to receive transcendent films like *The Tree of Life* and *Moonlight* as a gift. We may find our appreciation of God's gift of life expanded by the patience demonstrated by mystical filmmakers like Terrence Malick (*Tree of Life*) and Barry Jenkins (*Moonlight*). After reading *A Sacred Look*, we will come away with an expanded "must-see" movie list comprising under-seen productions like *The Painted Veil* (2006), *Gimme Shelter* (2013), *Calvary* (2014), and *Me and Earl and the Dying Girl* (2015).

2. Boyce, "Patron Saints of Cinema."
3. Ebert, "'Millions' Writer Wins 'Lottery.'"

Yet, Sister Nancy does not confine her cultural mysticism only to the esoteric. She is comfortable discussing the virtues of popular television shows like *Everybody Loves Raymond*, *Grey's Anatomy*, and *This is Us*. Her musical interests include massively popular singers like Kelly Clarkson, Pharrell Williams, Taylor Swift, and Chance the Rapper. As a parent of teenagers, I found myself most appreciative of her reflection upon young adult novels and film series like *The Hunger Games* and *Divergent*. Sister Nancy attends to the interests of teenagers with the patience and insight befitting a cultural mystic. She wants to understand how a controversial Netflix series like *13 Reasons Why* is impacting young people. She also is willing to reflect upon the fandom surrounding cultural events like *Star Wars: The Force Awakens* and *Wonder Woman*.

Throughout *A Sacred Look*, Sister Nancy dignifies humanity and celebrates the sacramental, real presence of God in our lives and in our entertainment. She extends the work of pioneers in theology and the arts like Father Andrew Greeley, Richard A. Blake, S.J. and playwright Karol Wojtyla more famously known as Pope John Paul II. I invite readers to slow down, take a deep breath, and enter into Sister Nancy's quite comfortable shoes. Patient readers will be rewarded with a sacred look at pop culture and may even find themselves becoming much-needed cultural mystics.

Craig Detweiler

Preface

E VER SINCE I BECAME engaged in evangelization of and within the media culture over thirty years ago, I have pondered the intersection of faith and culture, trying to name and describe that point of contact. Sr. Rose Pacatte, FSP, my mentor in media studies, initiated my quest to discover a theology that underlies today's popular culture through her insistent mantra that we, media evangelizers, must be critically engaged with the popular culture in order to become effective communicators in the twenty-first century. That stuck with me and tugged at my apostolic heart. I began to notice the subtle graces present there often without direction for a higher spiritual connection toward God.

The writings of Craig Detweiler, Barry Taylor, and Robert Johnston all piqued my interest in pursuing that connection of a theology of popular culture. Their masterful insight opened me to a view of the culture as sacramental, as a place where God's marvelous beauty is revealed. My readings led me to pursue a degree in Theology from Fuller Theological Seminary because of how they integrate popular culture and theology. This volume comes from those years of study, reflection, and much prayer. I discovered that in order to engage the popular culture as religious people, we must be fully immersed in Christ, the center of all life ✓ and history. Centering oneself in God is a mystical experience and a practice that one pursues regularly in order to engage the beauty and the dark side of humanity represented so often in a culture that seeks transcendence. To be a mystic requires a humble stance before God and the culture in which we live, move, and breathe. It necessitates a look of love, a sacred look, a prayerful glance that opens us to how God looks at each of us, poor, sinful creatures, but infinitely loved nonetheless. This is the beauty of faith. We do not need to have all the answers. We only need to know where to look for them.

Sr. Nancy Usselmann, FSP

Pauline Center for Media Studies, Los Angeles, CA

Introduction

A Sacred Look
–Communicating Beauty

I OFTEN CONVERSE WITH PEOPLE who experience an intense dilemma of how to connect faith and media for themselves and their families. Realistically recognizing the powerful influence media have upon our culture and each of us individually, they struggle with the desire to lead their families on the path of holy living amid the plethora of adverse media messages that are contrary to their personal and faith values. Pondering this quandary compelled me to find a theological underpinning to bridge that gap between faith and popular culture. Exactly how do we bring our faith into dialogue with the culture without losing who we are? How can we become holy in a culture that often points out the opposite? What type of anthropology and spirituality is needed for today?

New Mysticism for Today

I believe this calls for a new mysticism. A lived spirituality comes ✓ from a tangible, concrete experience of the Divine. To say we are spiritual without being religious is a farce of pop philosophy that eliminates the authentic response to a religious encounter, which is transformation. This means a change occurs in the person who experiences the One who is Other, the Infinite Creator, Being Itself. Mysticism, in its most authentic sense, is exactly this. To be a mystic one enters into direct communion with definitive reality but for whom that communion leaves the person changed. They live in the world transformed by their experience of the presence of God and communicate this presence with their redeemed humanity.

As the great mystics of the past, Teresa of Avila, Thomas Aquinas, Mother Teresa of Calcutta, John of the Cross, James Alberione, or Julian of Norwich communed with God within their physical and cultural context, so, too, are we called to bring that mystical experience of the Divine into our own digitally-sophisticated media culture and daily experiences. Being a mystic means being authentically who we are as believers. It requires a transformation on our part, as it has for every mystic throughout the centuries. It means not only to learn about God but also to personally encounter and develop an intimate relationship with God. As Christians, this means that we are to *be* the Gospel message that Jesus proclaims and make it incarnate in us. Our baptism calls us to this very idea of being the evangelizing word in today's world, preaching with our very lives the joy of knowing Christ.

Jesuit theologian Karl Rahner said that as disciples of Christ we are to live a *mysticism of everyday life*,[4] finding God in all things, in all circumstances and human experiences. It requires a moderate, selfless, honest, and courageous living always in service to others. He even goes so far as to express that the Christian of the future will be a mystic, or will not exist at all.[5] For us twenty-first century Christians, everydayness is a digital experience. I believe our call is to be *cultural mystics*, that is, the popular culture that pervades our lives. We are not to fight against it, point out everything that is evil in it, or condemn it. That is the easy thing to do. Instead, we are to be the mystics who look at the world with love and contemplate the deep underlying desires, longings, needs, and struggles present there in order to offer the world a message of hope, truth,

4. Rahner, *Karl Rahner*, 233.
5. Rahner, *Mystical Way in Everyday Life*, xviii.

beauty, and goodness. In order to do this, we must take a step back intellectually and reflect on the beauty that is present within the created world and in the creations of cultural artists who seek to give expression to the existential desires of humanity. It requires us to take *a sacred look.* Through this lens of theological aesthetics we acquire an anthropological-incarnational-sacramental foundation for a theology of popular culture.

Seeing Beauty

Seeing is a function of the body but also a function of the soul. The human person sees tangible realities and makes meaning that transcends these realities. This meaning comes from the depths of human understanding of what is being, what is real. To look at the real is to probe the depths of being. When we do this we touch upon ineffable realities that challenge and probe the human psyche to grasp a Beauty that is beyond itself, a Beauty that can be seen by plumbing the depths of created reality. However, this effort often meets with ambiguity since created beauty, even though its purpose, whether conscious or not on the part of the artist, is to point to the beauty of the Creator from whom all beauty originates, is seen through humanity's deformed vision that often becomes enamored and distracted by penultimate beauties.[6] Sacred Scripture and theology tell us that this vision can be deformed by the darkness of sin that can blind and obscure one from seeing the beautiful harmony of creation pointing to the source of Beauty, who is Being itself.[7] To truly see this reality, the infinite beauty of the Creator in creaturely beauty, one must make that journey inward, perceived, as Augustine says, through our spiritual senses,[8] to develop one's power to see beyond to the

6. Forte, *Portal of Beauty,* 11.

7. Ibid., 9.

8. For the full source, see Augustine, *Confessions,* X, 6, 8: "What am I loving when I love you? Not bodily beauty nor the gracefulness of age, nor light's brightness, so dear to these eyes of mine; not the sweet melodies of song, nor the fragrance of flowers, of perfumes, of aromas; not manna, nor honey; not

ultimate source. This interior journey allows us to understand that we, human beings, are not the creators or sustainers of life and reality. Instead, this interiorization opens us to a humble stance before transcendence, to that which is beyond our finite intellectualism, giving us eyes to see to the non-material, supernatural realities. This is the *sacred look*. ✓

Where Is Humanity Going?

Taking a *sacred look* at the popular culture begs us to ponder the needs of humanity. Early in my stages of religious formation, I would hear about the ideals of a young diocesan priest from Northern Italy at the turn of the twentieth century. His vision entailed questioning himself about where humanity is headed and how he can be a catalyst for good within the emerging media culture. Father Giacomo (James) Alberione not only contemplated the most profound yearnings of human beings, but he actually did something to help answer those needs and desires. He formed a religious organization that would use the most modern means human progress provides to preach the Gospel. For he knew with utter conviction that only an intimate relationship with Jesus Christ would satisfy the hungers of humanity. And the best way to communicate this message was through the means of communication that human invention developed, starting with the press.

Alberione knew that he needed dedicated workers in the field of communication to make this message consistent and enduring, so he founded ten religious institutes that comprise the Pauline Family. There is one burning question that he instilled in all his followers, "How often do you ask yourselves: How and toward what goal is humanity moving, this humanity that is constantly renewing itself on the face of the earth?" He continues, "Humanity is like a great river flowing into eternity. Will it be saved? Or will

---

the body so dear to the embraces of the flesh: no, these are not the things I love when I love my God. And yet in a certain sense I do love light and sound, smell and food and embrace, when I love my God, the light, sound, smell, food, and embrace of my inner being."

it be lost forever?"[9] This point of contemplation is always a burning question in the hearts of Paulines as it should be for all who feel the urge to do something good for the people of today and in the future. What kind of world do we want to leave to the next generation; one that is more confused and disillusioned, or more hope-filled and committed? This begins with us right now becoming mystics who live and work within the popular media culture in order to understand the most profound needs of humanity today and to propose a dialogue about how those needs are fulfilled in union with God. A mystic's heart, "needs to be more vast than the seas and the oceans,"[10] as Alberione challenges. Our pedagogical method, then, obligates us to start with an understanding of the human person.

Grace and Nature

Each human being is a recipient of divine grace because we are recipients of God himself as his children who are made in the image and likeness of God. Since we are heirs and offspring of the divine, "our kinship to God is not by nature and necessity, but by the freedom of the gift—by grace."[11] In this light, we see all as gift. All of being, everything in the universe and every relationship is a gift from a most generous God. We are ourselves gifts from a loving Creator and so are already disposed to giving and receiving.[12] The ability to receive the gift comes from grace alone. Philip Rolnick writes:

> The person who can receive the divine gift (grace) is more valuable than the whole universe, because the universe is a *what*, not a *who,* and the what exists for the sake of the who. Personality is itself the most basic and valuable of the divine gifts; it is the meaning of being created in the image of God. It is the unsurpassable gift, which

9. Alberione, *Explanation of the Constitutions*, 251.

10. Alberione, *Ut Perfectus Sit Homo Dei*, 455.

11. Rolnick, *Person, Grace and God*, 170.

12. Ibid., 168.

allows us to relate to God and to one another in freedom and love, and increasingly to appreciate that the universe in which we find ourselves is itself a gift of unimaginable generosity.[13]

The good, the true, and the beautiful are the essence of the ✓ gift—the gift of friendship and love. We can never fully exhaust their potential since humanity is always seeking *the more*. In our desire for ultimate communion and connection we find glimpses of this divine union in friendships where persons are gifts to one another. Popular culture offers examples, such as in the delightful Swedish Oscar-nominated film, *A Man Called Ove*. When Ove, the neighborhood curmudgeon, loses his wife to cancer and is subsequently laid off his job he seeks to end his life to be with his beloved wife once again. Every attempt however is interrupted because someone needs him. Instead of wallowing in his own grief, through his new neighbors he learns that not only do others need him but he needs other people as well. Such also is the example of the biographical romantic drama, *Maudie*, an Irish-Canadian film about the Nova Scotia artist Maude Lewis. Deformed at birth, Maude's family alienates her so she answers an advertisement for a housemaid to Everett Lewis, a fish peddler and farmer. Slowly their acceptance of one another in all their quirkiness leads to friendship and marriage, seeing one another as not only an answer to their personal needs and desires but as a blessing. Because we are in relation with God who is truth, goodness, and beauty, our self-gift to others emanates a living out of these very transcendentals.[14]

In Christopher Nolan's film, *Interstellar*, Dr. Amelia Brand (Anne Hathaway) tells Cooper (Matthew McConaughey), as they attempt a nearly impossible feat of directing their spaceship through a wormhole to discover alternate galaxies with life-sustaining planets, that science can understand most things, except love. They must choose to visit one more planet before returning to Earth and Brand wants to go to Edmund's planet, an astronaut who left years ago for this planet discovery and may or may not be

13. Ibid., 169.
14. Rolnick, *Person, Grace and God*, 184–85.

alive, but whom Brand loves. Speaking to her scientist shipmates for whom empirical evidence is paramount, "Love," she says, "is the one thing that we're capable of perceiving that transcends dimensions of time and space. Maybe we should trust that, even if we can't understand it." Love is a mystery since it surpasses time and space. It is that power within human beings that propels us toward the supernatural. It is ineffable. Authentically lived love is the core of an everyday mysticism.

Incarnational Perspective

Everything in creation leads us to a harmonious relationship of the beauty and truth of individual creations to the beauty and truth of the Creator, the source and summit of all beauty. This is the heart of theological aesthetics, in which, according to Hans Urs Von Balthasar, the main task is to cultivate the imaginative awareness to recognize created beauty as manifesting the presence and glory of God. This relationship between creation and the Creator comes together in the incarnate Word made flesh, forming a bridge between creature and Creator. Augustine says that the Word is the perfection of Beauty, the way we enter into relationship with ultimate Beauty through the "superabundance of his life."[15] Thomas Aquinas shows that it is in beauty where the Incarnate Word is revealed to humanity.[16] This encounter with God is an experience of grace working through natural elements. This anthropological vision makes the human person the starting point for a theological discussion on culture. For in the Word of God made flesh humanity now enters into communication with God in a concrete, tangible way.

Through contemplation of the Son of God made man, we encounter the eternal self-communication of God that draws us into a relationship of love, where the Word is the icon of the Father.[17]

15. Augustine, *Confessions* IV, 12, 18.

16. For his complete explanation, see Aquinas, *Summa Theologica* I, q. 39, a. 8c.

17. Forte, *Portal of Beauty*, 17.

√ The icon is how the Transcendent, the One who is completely other and not confined to limits, shines forth in order to direct the gaze of the beholder to glimpse the eternal.[18] Henri Nouwen implies that the icon of the Transcendent also invites the beholder into an experience of the Divine.[19] No longer is humanity trapped in its own existential darkness because through Christ we have been made new, as St. Paul says, we are a "new creation"(2 Cor 5:17). It is by this contemplative *sacred look* through the power of the Holy Spirit that we see Christ as the perfection of humanity, the One who shows us what it truly means to be human. Christ in his humanity expresses the truth, beauty, and goodness of God most unequivocally in his passion, death, and resurrection. For in probing the depths of human existence in its desperate, despairing darkness he brings humanity the hope of salvation. In the anguish of abandonment he communicates a communion of love. In the horror of death Christ offers eternal life.

By seeing the Word we see ourselves and we also see the One who is Other, the Trinitarian God who communicates the abundance of truth, beauty, and goodness. This Trinitarian communion of love is the communicative expression of these qualities of being that flow forth upon all of creation in God's self-communication.
√ These qualities of the true, the good, and the beautiful, these modes of being are often referred to as the *transcendentals*, meaning they lead us beyond material categories to the realm of the spiritual. Human beings are the receivers of this communication of God, but not passively or alone. Instead, this communication calls forth an active relationship of love—a two-way communication that gives birth to creative beauty in humanity expressed in its cultural artifacts that communicate the depths of human experience. This response does not remain only with the artist or the observer of the art, but moves beyond to the entire community. It is in grappling with what it means to be human that we come to an experience of the Divine. We, therefore, enter into that transcendent

18. Ibid., 75.

19. See Henri Nouwen's reflection on Rublev's icon in *Behold the Beauty of the Lord*, 20–22.

communication with God the Father aided by the grace of the Spirit, with Jesus, the Word made flesh, as our mediator.

Popular culture proffers the struggle to be authentically human. The 2017 Oscar Best Picture winner *Moonlight*, written and directed by Barry Jenkins, shows the life of Chiron in three stages—as a young boy, a teenager, and a young adult. Throughout his life Chiron is bullied and teased for being small and frail, shunned by his peers and emotionally abused by his drug-addicted mother. As a teenager, Chiron continuously endures the taunts of classmate Terrel to the point of being betrayed by his friend Kevin who beats him as part of a hazing ritual. He reacts violently and is arrested. In the third stage, we see Chiron as a young adult dealing drugs and going by the name "Black" which Kevin had nicknamed him when they were children. He receives calls from his mother who seeks to reconcile with him and asks for his forgiveness for not being there when he needed her. With an anguished heart, Chiron forgives her. He later connects with Kevin. This is a story about the human need for love. Can a child live without love? Can an adolescent learn about love when no love is shown him? In utter anguish the audience feels for Chiron and his desperateness in wanting to be loved. Is that not what it means to be human—to love and be loved? In our search for authentic human love and friendship, we ultimately seek to be accepted, cherished, and respected. In this search we yearn for the Divine—the One who knows what it means to be rejected and abused. When we reach down deep in our souls giving voice to those yearnings for love, we find the greatest acceptance in Christ, the perfect human being who "in every respect has been tested as we are, yet without sin" (Heb 4:15).

Sacramentality

Our communication with God takes place most concretely in liturgical worship and sacraments. It is through the communal worship of believers who embody rituals that communicate reverence, praise, and adoration of God that this relationship of love is clearly expressed. In the liturgy, the gathering of the faithful for worship,

Christ is present in his Word and Eucharist, thereby the believers enter into a profound and corporeal intimacy with Christ and his Body, the Church. Through the power of the Holy Spirit, liturgical/ sacramental rituals and symbols use material objects and human actions as means for encountering the Word made flesh, he who comes to redeem us and draw into a new and lasting relationship with himself. Through the objects of bread, wine, fire, water, oil, incense, icons, artistic images, and the theatricality of ritual, we not only perceive the Divine mediated through the tangible realities but truly receive grace, the gift of God himself, communicated through the material symbols and embodied rituals. It is through these symbols and signs that our *cultural imaginations* are formed. That is, the way we view reality and our place within the wider cultural experience, and in this case, the digital media culture.

When Doctor Ryan Stone, played by Sandra Bullock in the film *Gravity*, is stranded in a capsule at the International Space Station without fuel to propel her to the Chinese Space Station in order to return to Earth, she shuts the system down and prepares for death. One camera shot focuses on a small icon of Saint Christopher, the patron of travellers, while Stone is giving up on life. This symbolic screen shot offers the viewer a sign of hope, communicating that we are never all alone. There is Someone guiding and watching over us. Our liturgical communal practices represent that desire for human beings to belong, to be in communion. Though Dr. Stone is an independent, self-assured professional, she is also very lonely since her young daughter died in an accident. This is symbolized in her aloneness in space. It is through the communication with an Aleut-speaking fisherman on earth that she realizes then she needs other people. Her perspective on life changes even while she prepares for death.

The aesthetics in film and television often provide me with a spiritual experience, especially those regarding food. I love to cook so I notice the details in the *food movie* genre. Not only are the savory delicacies visually appealing, but also they represent some of the most profound yearnings in human beings—the need for connection and communion. To share a meal with someone is a way to get to know that person on a deeper level. Our cultural and sacramental imaginations are engaged when we see food in popular films since it provides greater meaning to the story. Jon Favreau's film *Chef* offers just such depth. When a particularly talented Los Angeles chef, Carl Casper (Jon Favreau), argues with his boss and restaurant owner (Dustin Hoffman), he quits his job and tries to make a living with a food truck in Miami with the help of his ex-wife (Sofia Vergara). Casper, who in the past became wrapped up in his work, begins to notice his son and his talents for social media when he joins Casper and his best friend (John Leguizamo) on a cross-country trip in their new food truck. The comfort food they provide on the truck draws crowds and becomes a catalyst for the sacramental moments of life—time with his son and a fresh start with his ex-wife. It is a story about communion and connection around the seemingly mundane necessity of food. Nonetheless, it becomes an inspired experience of reconciliation, forgiveness, and love expressed through taste, texture, and the beauty of satisfying cuisine—a genuine eucharistic feast.

Sacred Look

To truly *see* with new eyes, to develop that *sacred look* that sees beyond the cultural imagination and the tangible realities to a broader liturgical and sacramental vision of the human person, there is a need to become *cultural mystics.* This means we embody the desire for transcendence, that is, the desire to reach beyond what is tangible and surpass finiteness, while critically engaging the popular culture. We then can offer a perception of reality that is anthropological-incarnational-sacramental. To see with the vision of the cultural mystic means that we have a faith that compels us to recognize the profoundly rich image that the Triune God has of each person and all of creation. To embody the ideal of the *popular cultural mystic* is a spiritual exercise in recognizing God's presence in the world and especially in the artistic questioning in regard to human experience that ferments in popular culture. All Christians are called to be mystics, to *see* the world with eyes of faith. Pope

Francis urges us: "To enter into the mystery demands that we not be afraid of reality: that we not be locked into ourselves, that we not flee from what we fail to understand, that we not close our eyes to problems or deny them, that we not dismiss our questions." He continues that we can seek, "a deeper meaning, an answer, and not an easy one, to the questions which challenge our faith, our fidelity and our very existence."[20] Through a contemplative stance on the world and our popular culture mystics offer a transcendent view of reality fulfilled only in the beatific vision of our God. But it also offers us a way of bridging the gap here and now between our faith and our popular media culture.

20. Francis, "Easter Vigil in the Holy Night."

PART 1

Mystical Theology

Mysticism of Heroism
—A Cultural Obsession

I AM SURE EVERYONE AT one time or another in his or her childhood likely dreamt of being a superhero. I always loved Batman
and fantasized about taking a ride in that amazing Batmobile. I
also believed Wonder Woman was one to emulate. The television
show starring Lynda Carter had her fighting off evil criminals with
her lasso of truth and using her shield to dodge bullets and other
objects. The Wonder Woman movie offers a refreshingly new perspective in DC Comics's Extended Universe (DCEU). It is one of
the very few that have a woman as the central hero of the story.
Directed by Patty Jenkins and starring Gal Gadot as Diana Prince/
Wonder Woman, this story focuses on truth and love in the face
of humanity's darkness. Even in the midst of the hatred of war,
which seems to be the way humanity will destroy itself, Diana sees
that there is still an element of light and love within people. Diana
kills Ares, the Greek god of war, but that does not end the war. It
is only when she sees the goodness in humanity that her hope is
rekindled. Eventually, humanity's goodness wins the day.

Ironically, the central theme of this story reminds me of Saint
Paul's reflection about the apostle: "Take up the whole armor of
God . . . fasten the belt of truth around your waist, and put on
the breastplate of righteousness. . . . Take the shield of faith, with
which you will be able to quench all the flaming arrows of the evil

one."[1] Wonder Woman's shield protects her from evil and the enemy's destructive powers, which is exactly what faith is in the face of the Evil One intent on morally wounding human beings. Her lasso of truth induces her enemies to tell the truth, which Saint Paul says is the hallmark of a spiritual warrior. Diana's sense of righteousness and her authentic desire to bring peace gives her the interior strength to withstand the taunting of Ares. Fear is an emotion that makes one cower before a challenge or inspires someone with courage to overcome any situation. Courage is born from Diana's interior strength, just as it is present in any human being who rises above a fear-inducing situation. When I was a kid, I did not connect the Wonder Woman show to what Paul speaks about, but now, I think it says something about how to view this film and other superhero films through the eyes of faith.

Mysticism of Heroism

Hollywood seems obsessed, to put it mildly, with the superhero genre. Perhaps it is because these films fill the industry's coffers. Or perhaps it is because these stories are somehow integral to secular popular culture precisely because of something deeper that they reflect and communicate to the audience. I believe it is a mix of both reasons. Some questions and desires that these films stir in the viewer are our starting point for understanding a cultural mysticism, while looking at a mysticism that is incomplete or misguided. We can ask ourselves: What are the deep-seated and unspoken longings of the human psyche that the story reflects? How is heroism expressed in relation to the human person?

The Trappist monk, Thomas Merton, wrote about humanity's desire to rise above itself through its own powers as a type of mysticism secular society upholds. Wanting to be heroic is actually a good thing. It can be the impetus a person needs to act courageously and selflessly, such as one who jumps onto subway tracks in the face of an oncoming train in order to help someone who fell.

1. See Paul's explanation of an apostle in Eph 6:13–17 using battle gear for an analogy.

That type of heroism instills awe because many more people who may have been present did not or could not act in that manner. However, a heroism that believes that it is through our own abilities that we can conquer the world and save humanity is quite another meaning. Christ already did that. He does not need us to do it again. Merton calls this a mysticism of heroism.[2] It is a longing in human beings to transcend ourselves through our own powers and abilities. It is a spiritual perfection of and for ourselves,[3] and defiance in the face of despair. This type of mysticism focuses on death instead of life, since it cannot see outside this world into a future of hope beyond the grave. Is this the type of heroism superhero movies promote?

Looking at the popular culture we see humanity struggling to fill the emptiness inside, to desperately fill that bottomless hunger for something more than what this world offers. This sees our very perfection and salvation in something other than God Himself and, Merton would say, that is a mysticism that is implicitly naturalism, since it finds its perfection in something other than God.[4] This is not a seeking of God's glory but, rather, of one's own perfection here and now, an individualistic mysticism that focuses only on the self. Ultimately, Merton says, it is an escape from reality, since it turns a blind eye to the real and turns in on oneself.[5]

Superhero Obsession

A mysticism of heroism also makes us anxiously preoccupied since it involves transcending oneself through one's own powers so that it is up to each one individually to make things happen or to turn them around. Hence, the root of the superhero craze, as we can see in the many superheroes referenced as the saviors of humanity. Some poignantly dark heroes exude this mysticism of

2. Merton, *New Man*, 31.
3. Ibid., 33.
4. Ibid.
5. Ibid., 34.

heroism in a particularly violent, mercenary way. *Deadpool* and *Deadpool 2* present a character that is so opposite of what viewers emulate in most superheroes. Wade Wilson (Ryan Reynolds) works as a mercenary but was once a Special Forces operative. His crude humor and violent behavior are not about saving humanity solely, but are about himself. He exudes this sense of heroism that is self-centered and ultimately destructive, fulfilling himself by using others for his own benefit. Even though a view of collaboration and teamwork with other X-Men, Colossus (Stefan Kapicic) and -Teenage Warhead (Brianna Hildebrand), in fighting off the enemy plays into this story, it is ultimately nihilistic. And the "enemy" becomes muddled because Deadpool acts out of his own darkness and seeks revenge on the evil scientist who experimented on him making him a mutant who has extraordinary regenerative powers. His fight against evil becomes a twisted response coming from his own anger and self-destructive behavior.

Some other superheroes grasp a deeper understanding of heroism, such as Vision (Paul Bettany), an android created by Ultron, in *Avengers: The Age of Ultron*. Ultron (James Spader) is an artificial intelligence developed by Tony Stark/Iron Man (Robert Downey Jr.) for a peace program but eventually becomes overtaken by a god complex seeking to eliminate humanity from the Earth. When Vision confronts Ultron he tells him that he misunderstands human beings who seem bent on self-destruction. Humans are odd creatures, he says, that believe order and chaos are opposites but are really all part of the same reality. Vision reflects that with human beings, "there is grace in their failings." He embodies a more profound sense of heroism since he recognizes that humanity is worth saving. Vision's intention poses a selfless awareness. Saint Paul says that only true salvation comes through the order of love, of authentic freedom, and self-gift.[6]

The *Wonder Woman* film also expresses this deeper sense of mysticism. She wants to save humanity from the god of war who incites human beings to destruction. It seems at the beginning of her story that this desire comes out of a need to prove herself

6. Merton, *New Man*, 35.

a capable warrior. The setting of the story is the "war to end all wars," World War I. Princess Diana, daughter of Queen Hippolyta, learns the ways of the Amazons, a race of warrior women created by Zeus whose mission is to protect humanity. She rescues an American fighter pilot, Captain Steve Trevor (Chris Pine), whose plane crashes on the coast of their island of Themyscira. Germans follow him to the coast but the Amazon women fight them off as Trevor reveals that a war is consuming the whole world. Diana wants to go with Trevor to the front lines in order to destroy Ares, the god instigating war. As the story progresses, Diana learns what it means to feel deeply for someone and to care about them. She and Trevor fall in love, but then they both make the ultimate sacrifice—Trevor by giving his life and Diana by gathering up all her inner power to destroy Ares and to save humanity from annihilation. Self-sacrifice and self-giving are the hallmark of this story. ✓

Everyday Mysticism

I believe this film communicates something deeper. Perhaps it is not as self-centered as other superhero movies can tend to be. Wonder Woman's motto is that love conquers all. That sounds like Saint Paul, who in speaking to the Corinthians tells them, "Love bears all things, endures all things. Love never ends" (1 Cor 13:7–8). Christian mysticism is fulfilled in the giving of oneself ✓ in a surrendering love. It is about being interiorly connected, not agitated or anxious, but listening calmly and so acting serenely and fruitfully. Theologian Bernard McGinn says Christian mysticism is, "that part, or element, of Christian belief and practice that concerns the preparation for, the consciousness of, and the effect of what the mystics themselves describe as a direct and transformative presence of God"[7] in Christ. This is what will truly set us free from the forces of evil. Love of God and others is the formula for authentic heroism, not a self-serving mysticism. This is the contemplative stance to which we are all called simply

---

7. McGinn, *Essential Writings of Christian Mysticism*, xiv.

because we are children of God. And Wonder Woman, without the Christian reference, portrays this sense of transformation. We see how she grows in understanding about human nature, especially through her connection with Trevor; while at the same time she penetrates deeply into a lust for power and how that twists the person to desire evil. Her selfless behavior exemplifies true heroism that comes from love.

This type of heroism is closest to what Rahner would say is the mysticism of everyday life.[8] It is the experience of grace that grounds us in living out the call to faith, hope, and love— a universal call to human authenticity—something the culture craves. Anyone living courageously, lovingly, honestly, and self-lessly is fulfilling the integral call of the Gospels to love God and love one's neighbor,[9] since we cannot have one without the other. Even atheists and agnostics who live a selfless and generous life are giving glory to God through their attention to their neighbor. Heroes are not expected to be perfect. There is light and darkness that resides in each one because of one's own interior struggle between good and evil. Rahner would say that grace is experienced in the daily splendors and failures of life.[10] It is there where Christ's life is most expressed because his very everydayness instills grace at work. Rahner writes:

> That which is amazing and even confusing in the life of Jesus is that it remains completely within the frame-work of everyday living; we could even say that in him concrete human existence is found in its most basic and radical form. The first thing that we should learn from Jesus is to be fully human![11]

To be fully human is to be heroic. Maybe that is the heroism the culture longs for but only sees the excessive and imaginary as a way of illustrating a nascent desire that lives within all

8. Egan, "Mystical Theology of Karl Rahner," 45.

9. Mark 12:30–31.

10. Egan, "Mystical Theology of Karl Rahner," 46.

11. Rahner, "On the Theology of Worship," 121.

of us. Stories allow us to reflect upon our lives, our hopes, and our dreams in a way that makes this desire universal. Still, the very process of storytelling can muddle the message so that it only mirrors a self-centered culture that seems stuck in a narcissistic cycle. The truly redeeming stories offer a view of reality that has longer lasting effects upon how people relate to themselves, others, and ultimately to God. When the story does this, it lasts and provides a perspective of humanity that is authentically heroic—a self-giving mystic hidden in everydayness.

2

Transcendence In Popular Culture–Theology Of Grace

Grace as Gift

B EING A FIRM BELIEVER that popular culture can be a conduit
for experiencing transcendence, I was convinced of this once
again after watching the Best Picture nominee, *Brooklyn*, the
British-Canadian-Irish romantic drama directed by John Crow-
ley. The lushness of the script and the cinematography drew me
into a heart-felt connection with Eilis Lacey (Saoirse Ronan) who
leaves 1950s Ireland for new pursuits in New York. Her crushing
homesickness and longing for friendship coincide in a developing
romance with a tough Italian-American from Brooklyn. When
she returns to Ireland because of a family tragedy, life options
unfold before her that require her discernment. I was in the midst
of a transition myself when watching this and found new courage to make a hard choice, just like Eilis, in order to pursue the
higher good, that *something more,* which was calling to me. It is
ultimately the call to self-giving love. The struggle became a moment of profound grace.

Human beings experience the world in and through the self.
We become self-aware as we come to knowledge of the world
around us and develop language. These are functions of the non-
material dimensions of personhood. We exist in the world both

as material and spiritual beings since we do not exist completely immersed in the material. As persons, in the philosophical and theological sense, we are metaphysical substances while also being relational subjects.[1] There is a dimension of our personhood that is not influenced solely by the world in which we live. This is the experience of transcendence. Living as free, intelligent creatures we reflect on the transcendent realities of our lives and have hopes and dreams while questioning the ultimate purpose of our existence. To acknowledge these fundamental questions means we recognize that we are finally oriented to mystery. We are constantly seeking and searching for these transcendent realities that are beyond us and we yearn for that *something more* that they represent. These existential structures of self-awareness, transcendence, and freedom are present in all human existence, constituting personhood. An understanding of the human person, and the person's existential desires and purpose provide a lens with which to view popular culture from an anthropological perspective. This then will lead to a recognition of the supernatural existential[2] in each human being, that longing for *the more* that becomes visible through the symbols of popular culture's artifacts.

Personhood

At the dawn of the Enlightenment and into the postmodern era, humanity has seen an increase in denial of human personhood. Considering the extreme destructive forces of the two great world wars of the twentieth century along with the many incidences of genocide, we come to realize that an ideology that disregards human dignity lurks beneath the surface of human intelligence and power. When there is a denial of transcendence, as the postmodernists purport, then there logically follows a denial of the

1. For a deeper reflection on the meaning of personhood in today's philosophical context, see McArdle, "Ecce Homo," 5–7.

2. For the development of thought regarding the supernatural existential, see Rahner, *Foundations of Christian Faith*, 126–33.

concept of *person* since transcendence is essential to this concept of personhood.[3]

The market economy can also diminish personhood. Our technological consumerist society blocks human beings from recognizing the deeper realities of human existence because it focuses on a manipulated surface reality.[4] The television show *Mad Men* effectively portrays Madison Avenue advertising executives in the 1960s who persuade people to buy products they do not necessarily need as long as it brings in big money for the ad men's employers. It all ultimately proves unsatisfying, as in season seven's episode, *The Forecast,* when Don Draper dictates orders from his office couch for a campaign, not really sure that he has anything to say and feeling dissatisfied with life. The compelling impulse to consume, which drives popular culture, is what Pope Francis calls the "poison of emptiness"[5] that threatens true happiness. It devalues the person by insinuating fulfillment is found in possessions and profit. Consumerism treats the human person as a commodity reduced to an object, either one that is consumed or one that continually consumes. This limits the human being's freedom to seek the true, the good, and the beautiful, since authentic freedom is to actualize oneself as a person.

In our imaginary and sometimes not-so-imaginary worlds, this view of the human person naturally leads to dystopian societies where the destructive forces of our fallen human nature reign. Evolutionary biology dissipates the concept of the human person so that, "In the dismal view of things, love, personhood, and virtually all of human existence would be reduced to the struggle for genetic continuity in which selfish individuals seek to maximize their own little niches in a competitive and hostile environment."[6] This is poignantly portrayed in the film, *The Giver,* where society has become so controlled in a faux utopian community as to impede human freedom, love, and creativity. The young man Jonas

3. Rolnick, *Person, Grace, and God*, 6.

4. Gleeson, "Symbols and Sacraments," 11.

5. Francis, "Our Encounter with Jesus."

6. Rolnick, *Person, Grace, and God*, 61.

(Brenton Thwaites) is selected to be the Receiver of Memory and so comes into contact with The Giver (Jeff Bridges) who shares the secrets and knowledge of the past with him. This opens Jonas up to the deceits of the leaders and their control over human freedom and knowledge as a way of preventing war and destruction through new ideas.

The Christian perspective is that the human person is not fungible,[7] meaning that the human person is not interchangeable with any other similar or identical item. Each person has a non-transferable uniqueness. Just as there is completeness within the unity of the Persons of the Trinity, there is also differentiation in the relationships that glory in the uniqueness of the Father, Son, and Holy Spirit as distinct Persons in the One God. The human person's personality, then, is a uniqueness that cannot be replicated.[8] This is compatible with the concept of human dignity. Human beings are made in the image and likeness of God (Gen 1:26), and because of that have meaning and purpose.

Postmodernism's Denial of Grace

Surfacing in the 1930s, postmodernism as a philosophical mindset became all-pervasive in society in the 1970s. Philosophical postmodernism displaces the optimism of the Enlightenment worldview with a growing pessimism and wholly rejects the former era's perspective that knowledge is objective. It is an intellectual mode that calls into question ideals and values of the Modern era, such as the quest for timeless truth and an elevated perspective of human capabilities.[9] Postmodernism dismantles not only the intellectual constructs of universal truth, the human person in relation to the universe, and the natural moral law, but also denies the concept of personhood, transcendence, and ultimate truth, and so removes the very possibility of grace. Frederick Nietzsche, the nineteenth

---

7. Ibid., 55.
8. Ibid.
9. Grenz, *Primer on Postmodernism*, 6–7.

century nihilistic philosopher, developed an idea of redemption
√ where human beings redeem themselves. He called it the "gospel
of the future" where the will to truth is replaced by the will to power, in which values are self-created by the powerful.[10] This view has
become postmodernism's mantra.

The HBO epic fantasy television series, *Game of Thrones*
garners a large worldwide following. Created by David Benioff
and D. B. Weiss by adapting the series of novels *A Song of Ice and
Fire* by George R. R. Martin, the series tells of the peoples on the
fictional continents of Westeros and Essos. An epic saga, *GOT*
presents expert cinematography, acting, and setting, while telling
the story of the struggle for survival among the warring dynasties
that seek power to claim the Iron Throne and protect their people
and lands. The stories offer insight into the self-destructive behavior of these noble families who have created a world of distrust
versus acceptance, personal truth versus universal truth, murder
versus forgiveness. One of the most watched television series of
all time, these captivating fantasy scripts provide insight into the
√ postmodern creed, *there is no absolute truth, so my truth reigns,
for me.* Many critics judge the show's excessive explicit sex and
gratuitous violence, saying that it detracts from the overall story.
Based on happenings from the Middle Ages, the novelist says that
these stories portray what really happened in time of war during
that period. I believe the script's underlying postmodern philosophy and its political power reveals how power controls lands and
peoples. *GOT* expresses the angst of humanity that is the longing
for security and power, but it shows a power that unleashes the
dark passions creating excessive moral dilemmas. Through the
many intrigues and infidelities, the plot lines are interspersed with
sex that demeans the human person, a nihilistic view, glamorizing
the darkness in the human soul. Not everything needs to be explicitly laid out before our eyes, and in some ways, it is insulting
our intelligence. What the story supremely shortchanges is that
human beings become more fully human through the grace of
Christ. Although rape and violence are inherent in war, the show's

10. Rolnick, *Person, Grace, and God*, 99.

continuous plotlines revolving around such sexual violence only deface a human being rather than build up. It naturally leads to self-destructive behavior, giving the power of evil over the human person too much credit. Human beings especially are capable of choosing the good, the virtuous.

A challenge to Nietzsche's assertion remains: how can human beings redeem themselves when they are absorbed in the mire of fallen human nature? If they can possibly redeem themselves then why is self-destruction an ever-present threat and constant suffering so overwhelmingly oppressive? Obviously, self-redemption is a contradiction. Only someone that is above and beyond human nature can redeem human beings. Only a belief in God who is Creator of all things can save human beings from self-inflicted idolization. Nietzsche sees that power and violence are the law of life, as accentuated in *Game of Thrones*, however, the Christian view is that power and conflict are transient and that power can be the servant of the good, as is shown in the television series, *Madame Secretary*, created by Barbara Hall. Secretary of State, Elizabeth McCord (Téa Leoni), supports the education of women in Saudi Arabia by inviting the young outspoken Saudi woman, Noura al-Kitabi who was assaulted with liquid acid by extremists, to speak at an education conference in Washington, DC. While also halting further terrorist activities, Elizabeth discovers that the Saudis are after this young woman and she alerts security just before a suicide bomber enters the conference room. She helps to save the life of Noura and many others. The Secretary addresses major international threats daily while seeking the most humane and ethically suitable response. It is through love, the good that is directed toward the other, that power is elevated. Selfish use of power only leads to diminishment.[11]

11. Ibid., 134.

Grace as Divine Gift

Christian theological tradition holds that deep within the human being is an inherent tendency to evil that is activated through an immorality leading to social disorder and disintegration. This can only be healed by grace.[12] We have the ability to make choices, however, and we are capable of recognizing, even when violence and hostility seem natural reactions, the possibility of the grace offered to us by God to act in a way that appeals to our higher selves. Grace is God giving of himself to humanity. This gift of grace alone allows Father James (Brendan Gleeson) in the film *Calvary* to respond to a murder threat received in a confessional with supernatural forgiveness and self-sacrificing love. Grace does not diminish human nature or supersede it, since Father James continues to struggle with his own humanity. Rather, it builds upon it and is "an unsurpassable perfectioning of nature."[13] He continues his pastoral duties among his cynical and unbelieving parishioners while discerning the dilemma of his impeding death.

Grace is a foundation of the reality of faith. It is grace that exclusively mediates salvation, which is at the core of revelation. Through grace, God imparts himself to humanity. This gift of grace, of God's own life in the soul, means that something of God's light and uniqueness shines within the human person; and, in turn, when God chooses that person and acts within him, that person's own light also shines through.[14] Art has this unique ability to express that light in the grace of perseverance such as in the film *The Martian* in which the undying spirit of the human person is so expressly communicated in Mark Watney's (Matt Damon) persistence to return to earth after being left for dead on Mars by his fellow astronauts. His creative scientist mind allows him to find ways to perform self-surgery on his wounds and grow food within the base of operations on this barren planet.

12. Ross, *Anthropology*, 114.
13. Rahner, *Rahner Reader*, 176.
14. Von Balthasar, *Engagement With God*, 82.

There is a restlessness in the human spirit that longs for this supernatural gift of grace, one that cannot be attained by any natural means. No matter how much human beings long for it, this world alone cannot satisfy all our deepest longings, as is expressed in *Before Midnight*, the last of a trilogy of films created and directed by Richard Linklater about a man and a woman who met eighteen years earlier on a train in Vienna. In this film, they have become a couple and have twin daughters. Their conversation centers on their deep, profound longings and needs. Celine (Julie Delpy) tells Jesse (Ethan Hawke) that each of their personal fantasies and dreams of communion, love, and happiness will never match the imperfections of daily life. They will always desire something more.

The human need for grace is evident in the world, especially when we see and hear of destructive forces at work. If God were not active in human existence we would have destroyed ourselves long ago. Instead, there is the power of God's self-communication present at every moment, to every person, in every circumstance. That is the gift of grace. This grace is what gives us the ability to reach for *the more*, to the supernatural world, to what is beyond our material existence.

Supernatural Existential

The transcendental experience of our personhood is our starting point for speaking about God. Yet, there is another existential structure through which grace becomes present and that is the supernatural existential, the understanding that the finite, material world is not enough to sufficiently quell the deepest longings of our being. The longing for the infinite and the non-material is present in every human being. It is in this self-aware desire for freedom and transcendence that grace is present.

Based on this assertion, popular culture, too, can become a means for experiencing the transcendent. There is a pursuit for *the more* in contemporary television shows, film, music, and social media. We see this supernatural existential in television shows such as *The Simpsons* whose religious satire pokes fun at human foibles and religious practices while addressing issues of belief in the supernatural through its cleverly concocted scripts. NBC's television series *This is Us* continuously addresses religious and moral issues, often showing that some things are just beyond human control and must be left to the realm of the supernatural. In episode fourteen of season one, Jack (Milo Ventimiglia) and Rebecca (Mandy Moore) struggle in their understanding of one another as the fulfillment of all their desires. Only when a marriage accepts that each partner is fulfilled in surrendering love to the other, while recognizing that all their deepest desires cannot be satisfied by the other, can there be mutual understanding and acceptance of one another's foibles and yearnings. It is in the choices we make about those yearnings that make all the difference.

Our lived human experience leads us to seek that which transforms our existence into a life with God.[15] Everything authentically human can be an experience of grace—God's self-communicating love. This gratuitous love of God is what gives human beings the ability to contend with the darkness and weakness that overwhelms us. Humanity struggles with the angst of disunion, alienation, and separation causing spiritual disintegration and darkness. We address this angst in every era and throughout the centuries. Yet, the angst remains. When knowledge cannot answer a profound human question then often the arts are a place to turn to as a means to give expression to what cannot be fully communicated academically. Artists reach down deep in the human psyche and with sounds, images, reflections, tastes, and feelings express the inexpressible in order to give voice to the needs of humanity. It is often in the deep recesses of our beings where grace is at work. Pop cultural artists, then, are the conduits of grace if they let themselves truly experience and give expression to these existential anxieties of humanity.

15. Von Balthasar, *Engagement With God*, 13.

Receiving Grace through the Supernatural

When humanity is open to receive the divine gift of grace, there is the ultimate desire for what is true, good, and beautiful—for these are the essence of every gift.[16] Grace builds on nature. These transcendentals are present in creation and most clearly presented to us in Christ, for our relationship with God actualizes the true, good, and beautiful in us.[17] What is false and ugly is an entirely different category than gift, which is the opposite of gift since sin turns in on itself and cannot give or receive. We only give of ourselves and receive the gift of others in love. Love alone is what confirms the presence of these transcendentals in the human soul. Love is a mystery that surpasses time and space. It is the power within human beings that propels us toward the supernatural, the transcendent. Love is the gift of grace.

16. Rolnick, *Person, Grace, and God*, 170.
17. Ibid., 9.

3

Theological Aesthetics —Television As Art

W HEN I WANT TO relax and put on the television, I often find myself watching re-runs of *Everybody Loves Raymond*. Ray Romano, writer, director, and principle actor as Ray Barone in the series, shares about everyday experiences and the dysfunctions in family life. Being from an Italian background, I laugh heartily at the interaction with his mother, Marie Barone, played by the effervescent Doris Roberts. I relate to the realities of relationships, the struggles and desires that are expressed in the series. They touch upon ultimate realities but in such a comical way that the observer cannot help but smile at these blunders of humanity. Elements of the transcendentals in human interactions are present in the scripts that kept the series on air for over nine seasons and formed a generation of Americans. It teaches that sometimes we just take life and situations a bit too seriously. The creative arts provide the opportunity to think deeply about life, relationships, and beauty through the gift of laughter. And art opens the soul to deeper truths and the theological aesthetics present in television drama and comedy.

Aesthetics is a way of perceiving through the senses. It refers to the use of the faculties of imagination and intuition whose products are often poetry and art.[1] Alexander Baumgarten, who coined

1. For a more complete definition of aesthetics, see Viladesau, *Theological*

the word, said that aesthetics is "the art of thinking beautifully."[2] The word aesthetics is often referenced in regards to the beautiful or art that conveys a transcendent sense of beauty present in nature or in the human experience. Is the end of all art to necessarily communicate beauty, as some may suggest?

Some art is the pursuit of beauty but some art is about communication, expression, playfulness,[3] and representation of the deeper realities of human existence, and these are not always beautiful but can be painful struggles, intellectual angst, and existential yearnings. Many modern artists are in pursuit not of the beauty of life but the ugliness. Such artists as Picasso pursued a shock value that forces viewers to look deeply at the issues of the modern psyche.[4] Picasso, as well as Hirst and Pollock, have in some ways brought out the ugliness in art. Craig Detweiler and Barry Taylor in *A Matrix of Meanings,* say, "that ugliness served as a great metaphor for life in the modern world."[5] With all the horrors of war, the brutality of human beings toward each other that the twentieth and twenty-first centuries have produced, art often expresses this in rough, distorted figures and strokes.[6] It is an avenue of communicating the human angst and desire for *the more.* In this way, aesthetics can be a locus for theological reflection. There is beauty in art and that must be recognized and celebrated. Yet, how is grace present in the world? How does art represent the hungers of humanity for the spiritual? How is it a conscious expression of the transcendental tension between grace and sin? This is the role of theological aesthetics.

Aesthetics, 6.

2. Ibid.

3. Ibid, 10.

4. Detweiler and Taylor, *Matrix of Meanings*, 275.

5. Ibid., 276.

6. Ibid., 277.

What is Theological Aesthetics?

Theological aesthetics is the study of God and religion in relation to sensible knowledge, that which is art and the beautiful. In pursuing God, who is Beauty itself, the human being longs for the true and the good. These modes of being are what lead us to a relationship with God. In keeping with that idea, Hans Urs von Balthasar notes, if theology ceases its connection to and pursuit of beauty it then loses any ability to convince and persuade.[7] Augustine sees beauty even when its opposite is present, saying that everything can be seen as beautiful if is it perceived in God as the ultimate source. God, he says, can even be praised in darkness.[8] It requires an inner journey to perceive true beauty. However, Bruno Forte explains Augustine's perspective by saying that an ambiguity is always present when we perceive creaturely beauty because this can distract us from the true beauty of our Creator, to which all creaturely beauty should point. He continues to expound that we can have a "deformed vision" blinded by sin and so it causes us to not see the beautiful harmony in the divine plan.[9] God pursues us through the beauty that is his divine essence, so that everything becomes beautiful, since this Beauty who is Love touches everything. Forte says, "everything is beautiful, because supreme Beauty touches everything it loves, even when weak eyes or a heart wounded by evil are unable to perceive this Beauty's mysterious and fruitful presence."[10]

An entire network of interconnectedness exists in the world through this relationship of every created thing to the Creator. As Augustine relates, beauty comes to us and we move toward the Supreme Beauty.[11] The ultimate revelation is the eternal beauty becoming flesh, becoming perceptible to human senses. The Word made flesh offers the superabundance of life making a way for us

---

7. Valadesau, *Theological Aesthetics,* 12.

8. Augustine commented on in Forte, *Portal of Beauty,* 9.

9. Ibid.

10. Ibid., 10.

11. Ibid.

to gain access to the Supreme Beauty, the Trinity who is the source of perfect joy and beauty, and the way to salvation. Forte says, "The beauty of ultimate Love evokes the love of beauty, which little by little draws our inner selves to travel the path that leads to perfect joy in God, who is all in all . . . in beauty everything is made one, and all things find their ultimate meaning."[12] God's self-communication in the Word made flesh points us to an otherworldly beauty, an eternal beauty offering the complete fulfillment of every human desire. The pursuit of this eternal beauty nudges us on to see beyond the penultimate to what is of supreme attraction, that which fulfills all our deepest longings. Beauty is the very communicative dimension of love in the Trinity.

Theological aesthetics shows how the very realms of imagination, feeling, emotion, and art are where faith is expressed and so must be a locus of theological reflection. Popular culture, too, is the embodiment of religious experience and is the place where the popular and mythic dimension of life contains the symbols and rituals of modern existence. It requires, according to Karl Rahner, the hermeneutical task of interpreting the use of symbol and art as a theological source.[13] Popular culture is not only the realm of religious experience but also is an expression of the human spiritual dimension that embodies transcendence.[14] It is part of the human DNA to seek the supernatural, the Ultimate Beauty, the Divine. Art, Rahner explains, can be truly inspired and be a bearer of Divine Revelation, of God's self-communication through grace.[15]

Aesthetics of Popular Culture

If we understand popular culture as a means of God's self-communication and grace present in the world, then we can apprehend the culture's artifacts as a pursuit of that ultimate Beauty. Are these

12. Ibid., 11.

13. For a reflection on Rahner's theological view of aesthetics, see Viladesau, *Theological Aesthetics*, 17–19.

14. Ibid., 18.

15. Ibid., 18–19.

cultural artifacts truly art? If art can express the beauty and ugliness of humanity, the supernatural desires and the overwhelming struggles, the lofty hope and crushing anguish, then can it not also be present in popular culture? Many often consider television cultural art subordinate to the cinema. A cultural sociologist, John Storey, considers television to be "*the* popular cultural art form of the twenty-first century."[16] Art is creative storytelling, and television is storytelling that brings the audience into intimate connection with characters living through complex scenarios and human experiences. Some call this era the second golden age of television or the golden age of TV drama. The twenty-first century is witness to a vast development of television as a form of art, good art that brings a cinematic drama to its storyline. Some cultural critics, including Storey, see that cinema is no longer the defining cultural art form, but television has taken over and become a main influencer in popular culture. With the development of Netflix and Amazon creating their own streaming series, the major networks are no longer the only producers of some of television's best stories.

If we consider the television drama of the current century with the likes of *Suits, The Crown, Pretty Little Liars, This is Us, Orange is the New Black, The Walking Dead, Breaking Bad, NCIS* and all the spinoffs of these types of dramas, we can appreciate the influence they have had on popular culture. Television, many critics will say, is a business, with the advertisers as the deciding factor of whether a show begins, continues, or ends on any network. Since it is controlled by business, it has not proven to be a medium through which artists can truly express themselves or their craft. Armond White from the *New York Times* goes so far as to comment that, "Film is a visual art form and television is merely a medium."[17] Can the cultural artifacts of television still be considered art? Is television art that inspires transcendence and beauty?

There is no doubt that television creates some of the most iconic images of our times. It used to be only cinema that produced posters with images of the film, giving it cultural iconic status.

16. Storey, *Cultural Studies*, 9.
17. White, "Film is Art, Television a Medium."

Television, beginning with *The Sopranos*, has movie-style posters for each season, thereby creating defining images and icons of our times. One commentator notes, "The days of television as a second-ary artistic medium, in the literal sense—in terms of generating iconic pieces of art and design—are clearly long gone."[18] Popular art is art that reaches the masses. If we are to consider popular culture's art, what medium reaches the largest number of people other than television? Television has the unique cultural contribu-tion of connecting people from diverse cultural backgrounds and generations. It creates continuous storylines that generate topics for conversation and establishes communion. There are groups that had *Downton Abbey* tea parties as they gathered to watch the latest episode. Consider also the over fifty-two million people who watched the final episode of *Friends*. Social media's connection to television has also increased its popularity. People can tweet their comments and votes during telecasts for competition shows such as *So You Think You Can Dance* and *The Voice*, while shows such as *This is Us* have tweets going out during the episode.

Popular media art is multi-dimensional. There are several art forms being utilized in television. The length of the story is similar to reading a novel. The various episodes are like chapters of a book that keep us interested in the development of characters and involved in their lives, such as in *Grey's Anatomy*. We follow the personal and professional dramas of Dr. Meredith Grey (El-len Pompeo) and her interactions with the other surgical interns, surgeons, and various patients at Seattle Grace Hospital. Her on-again off-again relationship with Dr. Derek Shepherd (Patrick Dempsey) made her character relatable especially to women who look for that perfect relationship that will be the answer to all their longings. The soundtracks of television shows draw us in emo-tionally to the drama and allow us to experience the depth and feeling of the characters, especially in dramas such as *Chicago Fire* and *Chicago PD* whose emergency response personnel respond to extraordinarily dramatic situations with intense theatricality. The artistic sets and acting all draw the viewer into the story and make

18. Marks, "Is Television Now the Predominant Art Form."

one think and feel with the characters. Some cultural critics say that the complex narratives of contemporary television can now provide an enriching alternative to literature. Gary Holmes of *Mediapost.com* calls television, "the most vibrant and exciting art form of the twenty-first century."[19] Julian Fellowes, creator of *Gosford Park* and *Downton Abbey*, says of television that those who reject this medium of their time are basically doomed.[20]

Is Television Art?

Perhaps the question is not whether television is high art or low brow entertainment, but rather is it aesthetically pleasing and √ does it provide insight and deep questioning of the human experience? People today are discerning audiences and look for the art as well as the story. Granted, there is a lot of poor quality art and storytelling on television. However, there are quite a number of programs that wrestle with very serious issues and questions in society in profoundly compelling ways. Holmes reiterates that many television dramas express, "life-affirming inquiries into the human condition."[21]

Designated Survivor is an American political drama starring Kiefer Sutherland as President Tom Kirkman, an Independent who became president after the entire government body and every person in the presidential line of succession were killed in a bombing while in session. Created by David Guggenheim, this show deals with the conspiracies that led Kirkman to be designated as the president, while examining ethical issues that politicians face daily along with the responses necessary in crisis situations that pose the least amount of casualties. It often emphasizes that truth is always the best response. The same considerations are in *The Good Wife*, with Alicia Florrick (Julianna Margulies), a high-powered Chicago lawyer, who confronts legal issues with moral integrity.

19. Holmes, "Can Television Be High Art?" line 12–13.
20. Larsen, "Those Who Reject the Art of Television are Doomed."
21. Holmes, "Can Television Be High Art?"

Her moments of hesitation and weakness afford an underlying angst. The "God issue" often comes to fore in dialogue with her daughter, who is a Christian, while she remains atheist. The popular show *Stranger Things* follows a group of middle school friends who discover a government experiment that leads to supernatural incidences in their town. This intriguing sci-fi horror Netflix series' plots are riddled with metaphors and veiled references to Christian themes of good versus evil and the beauty of creation in a fallen world. It addresses morally challenging issues such as, sacrifice, forgiveness, authenticity, and friendship.

When *The Sopranos* aired its final season some critics regarded it as the greatest television series of all time. This American crime drama, created by David Chase, follows the mobster Tony Soprano (James Gandolfini) in his everyday experiences and lifestyle. In one episode, his wife Carmela (Edie Falco) struggles with her husband's constant infidelities yet she is unwilling to risk the loss of the affluent lifestyle that his business status brings her. It becomes an ethical and moral dilemma in her character. With narratives such as this, *The Sopranos* won over twenty Emmys and five Golden Globe Awards. David Remnick of *The New Yorker* called it, "the richest achievement in the history of television"[22] while Peter Biskind of *Vanity Fair* said it is, "perhaps the greatest pop-culture masterpiece of its day."[23]

Theology, according to Karl Rahner, needs to take into account the aesthetic dimension of life, of the feeling, emotion, beauty, and art as the primary religious language so that images and emotion are integrated into its discourse. This allows us, he says, to go beyond concepts and enter into the experience of the mystery of God.[24] Art is an expression of these human experiences that have profound meaning of themselves, but an even more transcendental connotation when taken from a theological perspective. Art, says Andre Gide, is a "collaboration between

---

22. Remnick, "Family Guy," line 37.
23. Biskind, "An American Family," line 3.
24. Viladesau, *Theological Aesthetics*, 12.

God and the artist, and the less the artist does the better."[25] So, can popular culture be a place for a theological aesthetic? In reviewing the art of television through its creative and sophisticated storytelling this cultural artifact can indeed be a place for theological aesthetic reflection. The human experience is the place of encountering grace, of encountering the Divine. It is the realm for creatively articulating the human realities and transcendental modes of being. Within this, artistic beauty gives voice, vision, and understanding to those emotions and experiences that cannot be articulated for the masses except through the sound, symbol, color, and visual art that is television.

25. As quoted by Detweiler and Taylor, *Matrix of Meanings*, 278.

PART 2

Anthropological–Incarnational–Sacramental Worldview

4

Christian Anthropology In Dystopian Worlds

Y OUNG ADULT FICTION TRENDS change as quickly as do popular music and movies. Many deal with the fear of a bleak future for humanity. Underlying these dystopian stories is a profound question that looks for answers. And that question is: Where is humanity going? So much of this question is based on how we understand ourselves as human beings. The value of the human person is the basis of a society that grows and flourishes. However, in the contemporary world the very identity of a human person is questioned, altered and disturbingly denied. This offers a bleak outlook on the future of the human race, as many dystopian stories creatively express in war-filled, tyrannical worlds where totalitarianism and dehumanization become the norm. How can a Christian anthropology offer a hopeful outlook to the dismal story of humanity that does not seem as far-fetched as at first glance? It begins with our understanding of the human person.

The Human Person

What exactly do we mean by "personhood"? This is a much-debated topic in our contemporary, political context, even though the concept originated in philosophical-theological debate around the concepts of humanity and divinity in the person of Jesus Christ, and has had significant development over the centuries. Grace is essential to the concept of personhood since gift is at the core of its purpose and fulfillment.[1] No human being creates oneself; we are all gift. *Person* comes from the Latin *persona* meaning a "face" or "mask" coming from the theatrical or public roles people played.[2] This connotation refers to one's distinctive individuality. The Greek word *prosopon* means "face" signifying that the face is something more than the physical surface.[3]

The debates in the early church focused on the term *homoousios*, meaning that God the Son, Jesus Christ, is of the same substance as the Father. This long-debated concept creates the core of our Trinitarian doctrine—God the Father, Son, and Holy Spirit—one God in three persons. The distinction developed over person and nature, for Jesus is one person with two natures—human and divine. The debate focuses on understanding *person* as a unique individual endowed with nature that gives each one distinct personality. This view only came about with Boethius using the philosophical term *incommunicabilis* that means each human person has a unique and wholly non-transferable quality. *Incommunicabilis* means that each individual is completely singular, distinct, and non-universal.[4] The human person's personality, then, is a uniqueness that cannot be replicated.[5] This is compatible with the concept of human dignity. Human beings are made in the image and likeness of God[6] and because of that have meaning and purpose. Thomas Aquinas brings together the concepts of existence and incommunicability by writing, "*Person* in God is the incommunicable existence of the divine nature."[7]

---

1. Rolnick, *Person, Grace, and God,* 7.

2. Ibid., 11.

3. Ibid., 13.

4. Ibid., 41.

5. Ibid., 55.

6. Gen 1:26-27

7. Rolnick, quoting Aquinas from his *Summa Theologica* I.29.3 in *Person, Grace, and God,* 55.

Christoph Cardinal Schönborn relates, "The world was made for man, but man was made for God. The true 'locus' of his dignity is to be sought in this unique designation of man, which makes him, in the midst of all other creatures, the living image of God."[8] He continues to write that this realization of the dignity of the human person is a liberating message and one that provides good news for the constant desperate seeking of humanity today.[9] Once humanity bases its dignity on a type of "pure nature," making itself the ultimate reality and finding an end in it, does it not then become destructive? Hans Urs von Balthasar succinctly writes, "Only where God is person is the human being taken seriously as person."[10]

We have created in our imaginations and somewhat in reality a dystopian universe where human destruction seems inevitable. *The Hunger Games Trilogy*, films based on the books by Suzanne Collins, show a society where the Capitol, a tyrannical dictatorship, greedily controls the way of life of the vast majority of its citizens in the outlying districts. The government assumes all the districts' resources to supply the excessively indulgent utopian society of the Capitol's citizens and enforces its power on the districts by constant propaganda, violent "peacekeeping" forces, and the Hunger Games, where the human person is only as good as his or her power to fight. Veronica Roth authored the books on which the films *The Divergent Series* are based. These also describe a dystopian world controlled by a totalitarian government desirous of a genetically perfect world. What it cannot do, though, is control the human spirit that defies oppression and control. These genetically altered societies, however, do not bring peace, only selfishness and destruction.

Popular culture's dystopian stories paint a verbal picture of the consequences of a nihilistic culture, where reality and existence are denied, and where God is removed from an understanding of anthropology. In a world where science dictates what is true and

8. Schonborn, *Man, the Image of God*, 40.

9. Ibid., 68.

10. Von Balthasar, *Von Balthasar Reader*, 194.

✓ governments attempt to quell human freedom, a battle stirs within each person. Despite the evil that lurks in human nature creating destruction in its path, there is always present the desire for *something more* that cannot be controlled or eliminated by any outside force. What is it that moves human beings to seek that *something more*? It is the power of grace, a pure gift that gives humanity meaning, the desire for the supernatural, the determination to seek truth, goodness and beauty. Is grace present in the dystopian stories of *The Hunger Games* and *Divergent* or does its lack leave readers with a sense of hopelessness in the sinfulness of human nature? The postmodernist denial of human personhood and the possibility of true altruism is present in these stories as well as how grace building on nature transforms a nihilistic anthropology by carving a path for a theological dialogue with popular culture.

Dystopian Worlds

Even though *The Hunger Games* and *Divergent* are two very different stories, there are many similarities that allow us to examine them in the same light of nature and grace. Both stories take place within dystopian societies under an oppressive government that came to power in order to quell the violence of an unchecked human nature. Both novels have a seemingly weak young woman as its protagonist whose power comes from sheer determination to survive and protect the ones she loves. Both of these heroines unexpectedly fuel a rebellion among the oppressed peoples, but also seek to prevent the spread of violence and destruction. Both sacrifice themselves for others out of self-giving love. Both stories cause their readers to consider the human spirit's will to survive versus the seeming hopelessness of a David facing Goliath. Both offer a reflection on the meaning of personhood, true altruism, and the reality of grace.

The Hunger Games follows the life of sixteen-year-old Katniss Everdeen who is the supporter of her poor family in District Twelve. Under duress, all the outlaying districts provide resources that feed the indulgence of the citizens of the Capitol of Panem.

Years before, a rebellion rose up out of the districts; the Capitol crushed the revolution, destroyed District Thirteen and made the annual televised Hunger Games the punishment of all the peoples. Each year, two young people from each district are chosen to participate in the death match games leaving only one winner out of the dozens involved. At the annual reaping, Katniss's twelve-year-old sister, Primrose, hears her name chosen. Katniss quickly volunteers in her place. Along with Peeta Mellark from her same district, she survives the games when, in defiance of the Capitol, they threaten to both commit suicide rather than allow only one of them to live. This action infuriates President Snow who senses this act of defiance is an indication of the rise to rebellion of the districts. Katniss becomes the symbol of the rebellion that ensues throughout the rest of the trilogy.

The *Divergent* series takes place in the post-apocalyptic city of Chicago and follows the experiences of sixteen-year-old Beatrice "Tris" Prior who finds her out of place in the faction society. The population is divided into five factions representing five virtues according to their personality traits: Abnegation (selflessness), Amity (peacefulness), Erudite (intelligence), Candor (honesty) and Dauntless (courageous). Before the annual Choosing Ceremony, every sixteen-year-old must take an aptitude test to determine the faction to which his or her personality most closely relates. Beatrice's test shows that she is *divergent*, having an aptitude for several factions, and finds out that this is a threat to the authorities that seek to eliminate all who are so labeled. At the Choosing Ceremony, each young person chooses the faction to which they wish to belong for the rest of their lives. If they choose a faction other than the one they originate from they are not allowed to ever return. This means they can never be with their families again. The motto is: *faction before blood*. When Beatrice chooses Dauntless over her family's Abnegation faction, she quickly sees the non-virtuous side of human nature and finds her hidden divergent abilities impervious to any serums given to control human fears, memory, truth, and death. A rebellion among the factions ensues and Tris is caught in a fight for the lives of her loved ones while risking her own.

Within both of these stories lies the question of whether humanity is destined to destroy itself or if there is something that prevents such utter annihilation despite human weakness for greed and power. Can the human person overcome the evil that is within while confronting the evil without? Can human love overcome evil and bring a sense of order and peace to a fallen world? How does a Christian anthropology provide an understanding of the human person represented in these stories?

Denial of Personhood

Postmodernism departs from the philosophical self-consciousness of modernism and purports a skeptical view of the arts, culture, authority, and religion. Through its denial of transcendence and ultimate truth, postmodernism has removed the very possibility of grace. *Divergent's* story is a Nietzschean view of human existence where the Bureau is the ultimate power that controls human genetics and human freedom. The people in the apocalyptic city of Chicago are part of the Bureau's experiments and those who are immune to their serums, the divergent, such as the protagonist Tris, are a threat to the "well-ordering" of their false societies.

It does not take much to see in our present-day society that human beings are unable to redeem themselves. If that were possible, why then is there still the ever-present threat of self-destruction and war? From this perspective, human self-giving is ultimately selfishness and love is self-centered. Can true self-sacrificing love be possible if human beings are nothing more than animalistic creatures following self-preservation instincts? Postmodernists view power and violence as the law of life. The Christian view is that power and conflict are transient and power can be the servant of the good, as in the case of Katniss Everdeen and Tris Prior, our self-sacrificing heroines. Love alone lifts humanity from its selfishness and directs power for the good of all humanity. Postmodernism's death of God only leads to the diminishment of humanity because once we remove God as a way to interpret the ✓ world then only unstable humanistic interpretations can replace it. For, "Without God as the sanction of human life, the high value of each person evaporates."[11]

We have the ability to make choices, however, and we are capable of recognizing, even when violence and hostility are the natural reactions, the possibility of the grace offered to us by God to act in a way that appeals to our higher selves. Grace is God giving of himself to humanity. He writes that, "The capacity for the God of self-bestowing personal Love is the central and abiding existential of man as he really is."[12] Yet, this grace does not diminish the human nature or supersede it. Rather, it builds upon it and is "an unsurpassable perfectioning of nature."[13]

Reality of Grace

Grace is a foundation of the reality of faith. Only God can be this foundation since he communicates himself to humanity as its ultimate salvation. It is grace that is an exclusive mediation of salvation, which is at the core of revelation. The very gift of grace is God's own ✓ life within the soul. When a person acts out of grace—the truth of his or her personhood—his or her true humanness shines forth after the image of Jesus Christ, God's Word spoken for humanity. It bears witness to God's life within human beings.

Though both dystopian stories do not refer specifically to the need for grace there is a noted restlessness in the human spirit that longs for this supernatural gift, one that cannot be attained by any natural means. Katniss seeks refuge from the oppressive experience of the Hunger Games and President Snow from which she can never seem to escape. Tris also desires a time and place where there is peace among peoples and no need to constantly fight against external oppressive forces that threaten to destroy human

11. Rolnick, *Person, Grace, and God*, 99.
12. Rahner, *Rahner Reader*, 187–88.
13. Ibid., 176.

memory and freedom. Both desire something that the dystopian world humanity has created cannot give. Categorically, it is the hope of freedom from constant battle not only with a particular group, as Tris says, but, "against human nature itself—or at least what it has become."[14]

In examining the characters of these dystopian stories we perceive grace at work, perhaps unbeknownst to the authors, but present in the anthropological representations. The first grace we see is the grace of creation. Through creation each human person receives the gift of life and is made in the image and likeness of God. As a result of this likeness, each human being seeks the transcendent and desires the transcendentals at the heart of their existential longings. Each protagonist goes in search of truth, goodness, and beauty even though they are often disguised or hidden from their grasp. And each one, toward the end of the narrative, pours herself out as a sacrificial offering that can only be inspired by the gift of God himself.

The second grace is the very gift of God in the incarnate Son of God. Without the knowledge and love of Christ we cannot grasp a redeemer who heals, restores, and shows a new way—that *something more* for which humanity longs.[15] For, as the author of Hebrews writes, "He is the reflection of God's glory and the exact imprint of God's very being, and he sustains all things by his powerful word"(Heb 1:3). This gift is always interwoven with human freedom and faith. Without explicit articulation, both of these stories address the ultimate desire of human beings for a Redeemer who knows what it means to be human and who understands the struggles and pains of life, but is also beyond it. "For we do not have a high priest who is unable to sympathize with our weaknesses, but we have one who in every respect has been tested as we are, yet without sin" (Heb 4:15).

Neither heroine can be that savior since they are broken and weak and often discouraged. They cannot heal others or prevent death or destruction, but they often notice something that the rest

14. Roth, *Divergent*, §11674.
15. Rahner, *Karl Rahner Reader*, 170–71.

of humanity cannot. They see the reality of love. And it is love that saves humanity from complete annihilation. It is love that opens ✓ one up to observe the uniqueness and gift of each human person. It is love that gives one the will to survive against all odds and offers humanity a future of hope. As Hans Urs von Balthasar would say, "Love alone is credible; nothing else can be believed, and nothing else ought to be believed."[16] Love alone *is* the gift of grace.

16. Von Balthasar, *Love Alone is Credible*, 101.

5

Christology In The Sci–Fi Cinematic Experience

I WAS RIGHT IN LINE with the rest of Star Wars fans when *The Force Awakens* and subsequent related films were first released in the theater. My childhood was marked by the franchise that catapulted the sci-fi genre to blockbuster status. To see the original characters return to the big screen was sheer pleasure, regardless of the storyline, as was evident when people in the theater clapped when Harrison Ford once again appeared as the legendary Hans Solo. Since the *Star Wars* franchise ruptured all box office records in 1977, and continues to do so, the sci-fi genre has expanded and developed to include many sub-genres including, fantasy, horror, time-travel, and superhero stories. These often harbor many deeply religious characteristics and Christ-figures, those characters who in some ways represent the life or attitudes of Jesus Christ. These elements are sometimes overlooked, but they have powerful resonances in the sci-fi movie genre in which humanity is seeking the desire to know more, to reach beyond what is visible, to push the limits of human intelligence. They spark our religious imaginations to help us understand contemporary society, and our values and beliefs. In doing so, there are underlying yearnings for redemption and reconciliation, often expressing a Christology for a technologically mediated culture.

Longing for Salvation

We all seek to be redeemed of this sickness that pervades us, the
sickness of the soul. It spreads through us no matter how hard we
try to ignore it or push it down or drown it out through activity and entertainment. This sickness is the sin that lives within
us,[1] as Paul notes, and is the cause of our dissatisfaction, disunity
within ourselves and with others, and this disconnect with our
Creator. There is the existential desire in every human person for
salvation—a salvation that promises something beyond this world
alone, that gives a reason to hope that this life is not all there is,
and that gives answers to the gnawing hunger deep in the human
psyche for communion and connection. Ultimately, the desire is
for love; Love who is God, Love who is the Person of Christ in the
Trinitarian communion of Love.

In humanity's search for redemption and salvation, only
one who is beyond human limitations can be that fulfillment.
Only the Creator, Being itself, can lead humanity out of its co-
nundrum of disunity and disconnection. God, the Father, sends
the Son to be the answer to humanity's desire for a redeemer.
Christ, being fully divine and fully human, shows us what true
humanity looks like. He shows us that it is possible to find eternal
beatitude and that God desires us so much that he seeks us out
even through the sacrifice of his own beloved Son. Jesus's paschal
mystery—his life, passion, death, and resurrection—is not just
one means of salvation among the many, but is the *only* way of
salvation. Our contemporary pop culture often unknowingly expresses this deep human desire for salvation and for a redeemer.
The current trends of sci-fi stories often illustrate this. One only
needs to watch any of the films of the *Star Wars* saga to see this
desire expressed in popular culture. Christ is the answer to our
most profound longings because instead of slavery and death,
Christ brings freedom and new life.[2]

1. See Rom 7:17 for Paul's in-depth presentation on how sin disunites the
human person.

2. O'Collins, *Christology*, 282–83.

In order to understand contemporary humanity's search for redemption as expressed through popular culture's stories, we will look at how sin effects human beings through alienation from oneself and others thus causing a rupture in relationships, a loss of self through death, physically but also spiritually, and an absence of truth and meaning in life.[3] These are elements present in the dystopian worlds we create in our minds but also in reality. Christ is the Redeemer who delivers humanity from sin and he is the love that heals alienation, death, and loss of meaning. Taking the philosophy of life present specifically in the *Star Wars* saga, we will understand how Christ answers humanity's yearning for salvation.

Good Versus Evil—Seeking Redemption

The *Star Wars* saga, created by George Lucas and further developed by Disney after the buyout of Lucas Films with *The Force Awakens*, centers on a classic good versus evil plot. The evil Galactic Empire was destroyed thirty years prior but now has spawned the First Order which seeks to destroy forever the New Republic. Luke Skywalker (Mark Hamill), the last of the Jedi, has gone missing while the Resistance, backed by the Republic and led by his sister General Leia Organa (Carrie Fisher), fights to save the Republic from being obliterated. A young scavenger, Rey (Daisy Ridley), joins with rogue stormtrooper (John Boyega), Han Solo (Harrison Ford), and Chewbacca in the quest to locate Skywalker and to reawaken the Force for the Republic's defense. Luke disappears after his Jedi-trained apprentice, the son of Han and Leia, went to the dark side and is now known as Kylo Ren (Adam Driver). Aspiring to be powerful like his grandfather, Darth Vader, Ren goes so far as to renounce his father and kill him in loyalty to Supreme Leader Snoke.

The series paints a dark constant struggle for truth and justice to win out over hopelessness and an abuse of power that comes through the control of the Force. The *Star Wars* series only hints

3. Ibid., 280.

at the presence of God through the power of the Force. However, much about the struggle between good and evil is scriptural and reminiscent of the apocalyptic heavenly battle between Michael and his angels and Lucifer.[4] Humanity longs for freedom from a ✓ tyranny that controls the cosmos causing divisions within creation. The Jedi are those heroes who are called upon to bring balance back into the universe, but, in many ways they are just as weak as others who struggle to overcome the darkness of evil within themselves.

What we see in this epic series is the human desire to break free from the sin that binds humanity to its own weaknesses and base instincts. As in the biblical perspective, "the unredeemed world is a world cut off from God and his life and given over to death."[5] There is the desire for a Redeemer who brings hope amid the suffering and grace in the midst of sinfulness. However, redemption cannot come from any human being or human creation. It can only come from someone who understands the human struggle but is at the same time above it. Jesus Christ, the God-man, comes to redeem the world through love. He is, "by his very existence, placed within the unredeemed world."[6] And not only placed in the world, but lives a human existence, suffers excruciating pain, dies an ignoble death, and rises again so that death does not have the last word. This is how Christ attained salvation for all humanity: sacrificing himself and his glory as ✓ God's only Son to be full self-gift.[7] It all comes down to *love*—the divine self-gift, for, "the only true Christian renunciation is the renunciation that goes with love."[8]

---

4. For the full biblical story, see Rev 12:7.
5. Durrwell, *In the Redeeming Christ*, 4.
6. Ibid., 5.
7. Ibid., 11.
8. Ibid., 13.

Sin as Alienation, Death, and Deceit

In the Scriptures, sin is first and foremost a separation from God that leads to death. Genesis illustrates how Adam's disobedience separates him from God by his being sent out of the Garden of Eden to labor and toil. This disobedience becomes our inheritance of which, "the human will, rendered weak and prone to evil, will remain permanently exposed to the influence of the 'father of lies,'" as John Paul II states.[9] It also brings death, as God pronounces a sentence on Adam that being dust he will return to the earth (Gen 3:19) and it distorts human reasoning and passion to the point of Cain murdering Abel (4:8). Sin enters in through deceit initiated by the serpent that deceives the woman (3:4–5).

The Scriptures repeat this same pattern of alienation, death and deceit throughout with Noah (Gen 6–7), the Tower of Babel (Gen 11), Sodom and Gomorra (Gen 19), Joseph's Slavery (Gen 37), the Golden Calf (Exod 32), Saul's Sacrifice (1 Sam 13), David and Bathsheba (2 Sam 11), and so on. Yet, God does not leave humanity to its own destructive force. God's merciful and unconditional love continually calls human beings back to himself desiring their salvation from sin's powerful influences.

Sin is the most acute alienation from God, self, and others. The Gospel of Luke in chapter fifteen tells us through the story of the prodigal son that sin tantalizingly presents a disordered love that excludes God. Through alienation from his father the younger son alienates himself, and in order to be restored to the family he must be restored first to himself, become aware of his sinfulness and separation from the community.[10] He deceives himself by thinking that separation from his father and the community will give him freedom and new life. Instead, his sin brings death. He squanders his money until he is destitute and dying from lack of food. When he comes to the awareness of his sin and how it has brought death and alienation then he experiences redemption. Life is restored, relationships are healed, and meaning is given.

9. John Paul II, "Sin Alienates the Human Person."

10. O'Collins, *Christology*, 281.

In *The Force Awakens*, the First Order has deceived the Jedi Kylo Ren into believing power is about death and devastation in order to have control over everyone and everything. By turning against all that he was taught in the use of the Force, he alienates himself from those he loves and who love him. Evil, in its alluring yet destructive power, holds him in its sway. Sin only brings disunity, deceit, and death. As long as there is love, there is always hope.

Saved by Love

The very life, death, and resurrection of Christ redeems sinful humanity from the power of sin and offers a promise of life beyond this world. And God's way of dealing with sin is through the weakness of the cross, says Paul in 2 Corinthians 13:4.[11] This is the weakness of love. We can only "believe in this victory of love ✓ . . . over everything which is not love."[12] This is the core of Christ's salvific work. Love alone saves. Love alone restores life. Love alone gives meaning. We are saved by love.[13] "For God so loved the world that he gave his only Son, so that everyone who believes in him may not perish but may have eternal life" (John 3:16). According to John, love is the very being of God (1 John 4:8). God's creative love climaxes with the redemption. Father O'Collins writes, "Love accepts, affirms, and approves whatever or whoever it loves . . . Love's approval entails the firm desire that the beloved should never go ✳ out of existence."[14] Humanity is so beloved by God that he offers his very Son to redeem us from the destruction of sin and offer eternal life with him forever. Only by offering his Son, Jesus Christ, can humanity be restored to right relationship with God. Only through his Son can we find new life and new meaning—"I came that they may have life, and have it abundantly" (John 10:10).

11. Ibid., 287.

12. Jungel, *God As the Mystery of the World*, 339–40.

13. O'Collins, *Christology*, 287.

14. O'Collins, *Christology*, 288.

It is the very person of Jesus Christ as Redeemer and Savior who restores humanity's very existence. The incarnate Logos who was the agent of creation itself becomes the mediator of redemption and divine revelation. God offers to humanity a way out of the dystopian realities we create for ourselves—a world of all that opposes what our existential desires truly convey. We seek peace, but only produce war. We desire loving relationships, but only find insecurity and disunity. We search for meaning but only find suffering and death. It is the person of Jesus Christ, truly God and truly man, who can redeem humanity from this dystopian existence. Therefore, "this offer of salvation is not primordially linked to a message, not even to a statement of faith in set truths. Rather, in a more radical fashion, it is tied to someone who is the base and origin of all these things: the very person of Jesus."[15]

Jesus as the Only Redeemer

The Scriptures express: "There is salvation in no one else, for there is no other name under heaven given among mortals by which we must be saved" (Acts 4:12). Jesus Christ is the only mediator between humanity and God. He is the only Redeemer and Savior. As Jesus is not one manifestation of God among many others, for Jesus is not one among many. Humanity is not satisfied with only partial truths, but we want assurance that what we believe in, what gives our lives meaning, what we live for is not a partial truth, but we desire to know *the Truth*, who is Jesus Christ himself. We enter into a relationship with the person of Jesus with our whole being, not just intellectually but also spiritually.[16] This is the truth for which we long, which we desire with all our might. We cannot make God in our image and likeness, as much as we would like to, but instead it is God who offers humanity salvation, freely. He pays the price. Humanity is the receiver of God's pure, loving gift. And this salvation is a gift that extends beyond human beings into

15. Ladaria, *Jesus Christ Salvation of All*, 74.
16. Ibid., 67–69.

all creation for it is, "the realization of God's cosmic design to be brought about in his Son, Jesus Christ—a project that began with creation and that is to be fulfilled in the *parousia*."[17]

Sci-Fi Seeks Redemption

The *Star Wars* stories present one oppressive force after another that hold human beings captive to their distorted human nature and attempt to manipulate them to the dark side of the Force. There seems to be no way out. Yet, in the films, we see several of the characters, specifically the protagonist Rey, and before her Luke Skywalker, continually fight for intellectual, physical, and spiritual freedom, as they grapple with the consequences of their own fallen human nature. Sin, shown as the opposite of the Jedi's virtues, cannot be held at bay unless each person is willing to resist the evil that lives within them. Darth Vader and his grandson Kylo Ren played to the lure of evil's power, so much so that it consumed them. Yet, the desire for redemption is a glimmer of light in the soul. At the end of *Return of the Jedi,* Vader saves Luke's life by throwing the Emperor down into the Death Star's core. The evil power from the Force's dark side is unleashed striking Vader and mortally wounding him. His redemption was that act of self-sacrifice, giving of himself so his son may live. Sin, guilt, pain, and suffering are part of human existence that seeks redemption. It is that spark of the supernatural in every human being that desires the good. The Force holds the power for good, for self-gift, for love, if we choose it. Symbolically, these stories answer the question of who will redeem us from this sin that oppresses us, as Paul so aptly describes in his Letter to the Romans (Rom 7:23). As Christians, we know the answer, the one who is both Creator and Redeemer, the One in whom the *Force* resides. Christ alone.

Without a Redeemer the struggle between good and evil within us would destroy us. There would be no reason to resist the darkness that sometimes pervades our human existence. But,

17. Ibid., 71.

because there is a Redeemer who transcends this struggle, who conquers death, sin, and evil once for all, we can have hope. Human beings innately know this. We seek freedom from this war both inside of us and around us, as the Jedi know too well. Christ sets humanity free from sin's oppression for, "the death he died, he died to sin, once for all; but the life he lives, he lives to God" (Rom 6:10). And because Christ put sin to death, we too, no longer present our members as instruments of wickedness, but rather we present ourselves to God as those who have been brought from death to life (Rom 6:13). No longer do we live as those who are oppressed, but we have been given new life through Jesus Christ our Savior and Redeemer, for he has set us free from the law of sin and death (Rom 8:2), and offers not a dystopian view of life but a true, joyous, and hopeful promise of life with him for all eternity.

6

Expressing the Mystery—
Sacramental Imagination
In Film

O NE OF MY FAVORITE pastimes is to wander around art muse-
ums. I am always fascinated by the artists' use of symbols to
convey some profound meaning of human existence. Rembrandt's
use of light shining on a face, illuminating the subject from within
shows reflective thought and intelligence, such as in his *Old Man
in Military Costume* as well as awareness and righteousness in
Daniel and Cyrus before the Idol Bel. The light hues are contrasted
with the intensely dark backgrounds that symbolize the power of
light to pierce the darkness—physically but also spiritually. Viewing digital media arts requires the same reflection and attention to
detail. Symbols in contemporary film and television shows offer
the observer a rich viewing experience when these symbols are
understood, grasped, and contemplated.

Human beings, as transcendent beings, are oriented to mystery, to the supernatural. We were born in mystery and directed to
mystery. Karl Rahner says that the human person, "is the question
to which there is no answer."[1] This, however, does not mean that
all of human existence is wrapped in uncertainty, but rather that
the answers we attempt to make about our fundamental existential

---

1. Rahner, *Content of* Faith, 73.

questions leave us only with more questions rather than answers.
We are ultimately striving for communion with the supernatural, the other, who is God. This God we are ultimately oriented to is incomprehensible. Rahner explains:

> The human person is the unanswerable question. His fulfillment and happiness are the loving and worshiping acceptance of his incomprehensibility, in the love of God's incomprehensibility with which we can learn to "cope" only by the practice of love and not by the theory of the desire to understand.[2]

Love is that which allows us to surrender our control of understanding the fulfillment of the human person and everything else to the incomprehensibility of God who is Love Itself. Mystery is not about that which we cannot know but rather about what we cannot transcend or exhaust. It is endlessly intelligible.[3]

Liturgy and Sacraments

Since the spiritual is wrapped in mystery there is need for us finite beings to *see* the expression of God's presence in the created world through tangible and material substances. The Church's sacraments and liturgy are concrete communal expressions of the presence of God in creation.[4] Liturgical worship is the embodiment of created reality offering an act of worship of its Creator. Sacraments, through liturgical ritual, make grace perceptible. A *sacrament* is often defined in Augustine's terms as a "visible sign of invisible grace" or a "sacred sign" that makes the sacred visible. This concept of sacrament can be understood in a much wider context than the connotation of the Seven Sacraments of the Church. It can also be understood as meaning that all that is visible holds the potential

2. Ibid., 80.

3. O'Donovan, *World of Grace*, 40.

4. Eggemeier, *Sacramental-Prophetic Vision*, 9.

to be a sign of the sacred, all human experience can be the place where God is present.[5]

The purpose of sacraments is to not simply mediate grace, but to transform human existence. Richard McBrien states, "A sacramental perspective is one that 'sees' the divine in the human, the infinite in the finite, the spiritual in the material, the transcendent in the immanent, the eternal in the historical."[6] The broader understanding of sacrament, then, encompasses all of human experience that reaches for *transcendence* or *the more*. Rahner says that nothing is finished or fully created until it becomes a sacrament— a coming together of the natural with the supernatural. Christ effected a change in humanity, he says, and his humanity is the very visibility of God.[7] Christ is the perfect sacrament and through Christ the entire created order is made sacramental. As Henri de Lubac quotes, it is a "sensible bond between two worlds"[8]—the world of visibility and the world of God coming together in a sacrament. He says the, "Sacramental reality is not just any sign, which is provisional and can be changed at will . . . It is always through it that we reach what it signifies; it can never be superseded, and its bounds cannot be broken."[9]

Sacraments employ symbols and signs that convey a depth of meaning. A sign specifically points to something beyond itself and communicates a sense that is deeper than the concrete object that it is. A symbol is a type of sign that often has numerous connotations and reaches beyond the sign itself to touch the imagination and emotions as a way of communicating feelings and ideas.[10] Concrete objects contain invisible dimensions that are not immediately sensible to human experience. There are layers of meaning. "'To live' a symbol and to decipher the messages correctly is equivalent to gaining access to the universal. To transform

---

5. Gleeson, "Symbols and Sacraments," 1.

6. McBrien, *Catholicism*, 9–10.

7. Rahner, *Theologian of Graced Search*, 281.

8. de Lubac, *Splendor of the Church*, 202.

9. Ibid., 203–4.

10. Gleeson, "Symbols and Sacraments," 2.

an individual experience by symbolism is equivalent to opening it to the Spirit."[11] Symbols can take us to the depths of things and so can be experienced through contemplation and reflection. When we bring this sacramental imagination to the art of popular culture we break open this symbolism and reach through the transparent layers to discover the hungers of humanity and the desire for the supernatural. In *A Wounded Innocence*, Alejandro Garcia-Rivera says, "The beautiful is not necessarily the 'pretty' or the 'pleasing.' I believe the beautiful is not simply a quality that is self-evident or a judgment of taste but a reality, indeed a community, being discovered and evolving."[12]

We transcend the limits of our finite existence to the domain of the Divine. We reach over our present experience to touch the Divine Reality, God who is Creator of all that is, the ultimate desire of all human longings. This anthropological view is the very human basis for what is called sacramentality.[13]

Sacramentality

When we enter into the realm of mystery, and of God, the incomprehensible, we seek symbols and signs to give expression to our experiences, our emotions, and our awareness. These expressions are sacramental since they make the invisible God visible. But, it requires a certain awareness to recognize God present in human experience. This is a "sacramental awareness"[14] and is often the way of artists, poets, and musicians, since it requires an acceptance of mystery while seeking to convey this through emotions and human expressions.

Sacramentality involves images as symbols and signs that need our contemplation, not necessarily our decoding. We look at

11. Eliade, *Symbolism, the Sacred & the Arts*, 13.

12. Garcia-Rivera, *Wounded Innocence*, 11.

13. Gleeson, "Symbols and Sacraments," 2.

14. Ibid., 9.

art and ask what it desires of us, not what it *means*.[15] It is the same with sacraments and sacramentality. We discover not what they mean but what they convey—the presence, the gift, the grace. By employing theological aesthetics we go deeper into the sacraments' effects and do not remain at their surface meaning. This divine life we receive in the sacraments is that *more* that we seek, that desire in the human consciousness for what is beyond our material reach. The symbols in liturgical rituals bring us beyond the surface of the materiality to the greater depth of its supernaturality. As it says in Genesis 1:31, "God saw all that he had made, and indeed, it was very good." This is the very sacramentality of creation.

The core of sacramentality is the use of symbols and signs to convey deeper realities. So as I said, signs direct us to something beyond themselves. Symbols are complex signs that convey a series of meanings and indicate their depth. They allow us to see beyond, to feel deeply, and to contemplate.[16] Artists often think symbolically and have a peculiar sacramental awareness that many people do not possess. Artists tend to reach toward mystery, the unexplainable, and the existential. They extend toward feeling, sensitivity, reflective cognition that enters into the mystery while reflecting on human experience. John Shea explains, "Sacramental consciousness does not desert the concrete, historical world but turns it into a symbol."[17] Poets do this with language. In his poem *God's Grandeur*, Gerard Manley Hopkins sees the beauty present in nature and exclaims, "The world is charged with the grandeur of God. It will flame out, like shining from shook foil." He observes God's presence that shines forth with brilliancy more than natural light can convey. He sees the sacramentality present in creation, in the light flickering off the leaves of trees, in nature's wondrous beauty only to reflect the even more beauteous wonder of God's brilliance.

The sacramental awareness is ingrained in such master artists as DaVinci, Carravaggio, Cezanne, Matisse, John Singer Sargent,

15. Garcia-Rivera, *Wounded Innocence*, 15.
16. Gleeson, "Symbols and Sacraments," 2.
17. Shea, *Stories of God*, 21.

Wassily Kandinsky, and Georgia O'Keefe, as well as in contemporary artists such as Jay DeFeo and Jasper Johns. It is also present in filmmakers such as Lasse Hallstrom, John Curran, and Christopher Nolan. Alfonso Cuarón, director of *Children of Men* the British-American dystopian thriller, expressly shows the sacramental through rich symbolism in the story of the desperation of humanity that, after eighteen years of global infertility, is on the brink of extinction. Theo (Clive Owen) becomes an unlikely hero when he helps a pregnant immigrant, Kee (Clare-Hope Ashety) escape from the Fishes, the militant immigrant rights group. They make it to the ship *Tomorrow* that leads to an island where scientists of the "Human Project" work out solutions to infertility. Hope is symbolized in the sound of a baby crying, the light shining into an abandoned elementary school, and the image of children in family photos. Terrance Malick, too, employs the sacramental in his films. His epic art film, *The Tree of Life,* blends the story of a young boy named Jack who grows up in 1950s Texas, learning and growing into life's deeper meaning, with the imagery of the creation of the universe and the beginning of life on Earth. It is a poetic reflection on the mystery of God and of grace active in our lives. It is through symbol that deeper meaning is conveyed. It is through nature that grace is made visible. It is in our sacramental imaginations that God's presence is touched in human experience.

Sacramental Imagination

Sacramentality is seeing the presence of God in the world and in all human experience. It takes our imagination to move beyond the signs and symbols to the deeper meaning they express—to the point that everyday experiences, situations, objects, and persons are, "revelations of grace."[18] The Seven Sacraments of the Church give actual grace. Popular culture's artifacts, such as film, music, and graphic art, can provide grace-filled moments. Robert Johnston says, "We are . . . provided with an occasion for encountering

18. Greeley, *Catholic Imagination*, 1.

our Lord afresh, as God transforms the stuff of life into a sacramental that reveals briefly, yet indelibly, something of his glory and grace."[19] Today cultural artifacts can be a channel of God's self-communication and engage our *sacramental imagination*.[20]

What then do we mean by sacramental imagination? In the action of the form of the sacrament is the sacramentality and it is God who takes the first action. For it is God's covenantal faithfulness that is, "the motivating force of sacramentality that overcomes any ministerial deficiency."[21] That which allows us to participate in this divine life of God is our very *sacramental imagination*. This is the way of viewing reality through the lens of faith where the finite mediates the infinite and all of creation can be a mediation of grace.[22]

Our human faculty of imagination is the ability to form mental images in our minds of things we have not experienced through our senses. A sacramental imagination means that we can experience creation as a manifestation of God,[23] allowing us to see beyond the physical to the supernatural. All of reality reveals the presence of God. It is seeing the tangible realities as communicating deeper meaning and purpose. It is an incarnational perspective of the world and human experience.

These are sacramental moments in human existence and God's grace is active in the world through the many longings and desires of humanity. Sacramental imagination refers to the everyday events, persons, situations, and experiences that are moments of God's self-communication—moments that reveal God's grace. These sacramentals make God's presence known, not just an idea of God, and so are revelations of grace at work in the world. They make God present in our midst, this God who created all things. His presence permeates all of creation and communicates the beauty and goodness of God.

19. Johnston, "Visual Christianity," 181.

20. Ibid., 1.

21. Ibid., 16.

22. Ibid., 16.

23. Ibid., 8.

The Sacramental in Cinema

The cultural art of cinema provides numerous examples of sacramental imagination at work. Culinary feasts deliver a wealth of symbolism representative of the Eucharist liturgy, such as in the lush presentation director Lasse Hallstrom offers in *The Hundred-Foot Journey*. The rich symbolism of food is the catalyst for understanding and acceptance amid cultural clashes. An Indian family moves from Mumbai to a small town in France to open a restaurant directly across the street from a renowned Michelin-star winning restaurant, owned by Madame Mallory (Helen Mirren). After fierce competition for acceptance, it is the tastes and sights of rich cuisine that provide the opportunity for reconciliation and collaboration.

The perseverance of married love, one that does not give up on one another despite severe trials, is aptly symbolized in the repetition of rituals in *The Painted Veil*. This third adaptation of the 1925 novel by W. Somerset Maugham and directed by John Curran, has bacteriologist Walter Fane (Edward Norton) marry Kitty Garstin (Naomi Watts) and move to Shanghai where he studies infectious diseases. She marries only to get as far away as possible from her overbearing mother, finding herself unsuited to Walter and involving herself with Charles Townsend (Liev Schreiber) in a passionate relationship. When Walter learns of the affair he takes Kitty to a remote mountainous village in China to treat victims of cholera. While there, Kitty volunteers at an orphanage run by French nuns. Slowly, through the innocence of the children she serves, her own "innocence" returns and she begins to appreciate her husband—the beauty of her marriage vows and his selflessness in his work. The beauty of marriage is shown through self-gift and its lack when selfishness supersedes.

Christopher Nolan's sci-fi crime thriller *Inception* is the story of Dominick Cobb (Leonardo DiCaprio), a professional thief who commits espionage by entering the subconscious of the human targets so as to extract valuable information for a heist. He is a master at infiltrating his victim's dreams in order to manipulate information. Cobb then is offered a chance to erase all his past criminal activity as payment for inception, the implanting of ideas into another person's subconscious. The film shows how twisted one's conscience becomes when warped by criminal activity, yet there is the yearning in Cobb for happiness and release from being trapped in the dream world. The spinning of the totem, a consistent symbol throughout the film, shows the continuance of time regardless of the actions of a dream world. The totem is a test of reality. It spins indefinitely in the dream world, but falters and stops in reality. Time, as this life, has an end. Eternity lasts forever. And that cannot be controlled or manipulated like dreams. Authentic love of family and hope beyond what this world can offer, symbolize eternal life as is shown when Cobb finally sees his children again.

August Wilson's movie script based on his stage play, *Fences*, offers an abundance of symbols that give depth of meaning to the entire film. Directed by Denzel Washington who also plays the lead character, Troy Maxson, the film takes place in 1950s Pittsburgh. Troy, a sanitation worker, lives with bitterness about his unfulfilled dreams of becoming a professional baseball player. He was too old by the time Major League Baseball allowed African-Americans to participate. His wife Rose (Viola Davis) asks Troy to build a fence around their property taking him years to complete. The fence becomes a symbol of security, protection, and safety for the family. But, it also represents each person's inner confinement, especially Troy's. With all his rigidity and hardness holding everyone else tightly in the fence, he becomes the one who steps out of the fence through his infidelity. The scene of Rose and Troy arguing about his unfaithfulness is shot through the holes of the fence conveying the complexities of the human person in all its varied emotions and excuses. It provides a framework from which to evaluate the entire film.

Mediation of Grace

What the sacramental imagination expresses is that sacramentality revolves around mediation. The non-material is mediated through the material. The sacraments are mediated through symbols. Transcendence is mediated through immanence. God the Father is mediated through the Incarnate Son. Christ Jesus not only mediates the presence of God but also is God's very self-communication. He is grace. He is salvation. He is justification. Jesus Christ is the perfect sacrament that transmits actual grace upon believers, the gift of himself. Sacramental imagination is grounded in a creation-incarnation-resurrection paradigm of practical theology. It is through the natural created world that God's grace is mediated. It is in the person of Jesus, God's Son who is God's life to humanity, and in his resurrection that all is confirmed by the greatest act of divine intervention in creation. For, "The saving grace that God makes available to us in and through creation is the gift of divine love that exceeds even our wildest hope."[24] It is precisely this view of the structure of creation where we think differently about the material and finite, seeing them as access points to experience the infinite beauty and goodness of God mediated through the finite.[25] This is what makes a *sacramental imagination*.

Effective cultural mystics are those who can interpret the common human experience in the light of the great mysteries of faith using the symbols present in the natural world to illuminate our spiritual experiences. It is precisely these common everyday symbols that point to, or reveal, deeper realities that can be means of grace. Popular culture's use of these symbols and signs provide an understanding of our human experience and purpose. Signs convey meaning guiding us to the mystery. They engage our imaginations to reflect upon the spiritual realm, the *supernatural existential*. Concrete objects and embodied rituals contain invisible dimensions that are not immediately sensible to human experience. There are layers of meaning. When we bring this

24. Shea, *Stories of God*, 24.
25. Ibid., 24.

sacramental/liturgical imagination to the artifacts of popular culture we break open this symbolism and reach through the perhaps not-so-transparent layers to discover the hungers of humanity and the desire for the supernatural.\

7

Catholic Cinematic Imagination

W E CAN OFTEN TAKE for granted that our worldview is shaped and molded by our childhood experiences. So much of who we are is a conglomeration of our ancestral history, parental wisdom, ethnic heritage, and youthful existences. The joys and excitement as well as the pains and anxieties of family living fashion us into the people we have become. As a Roman Catholic with a German-Italian heritage, I realize how that has formed my cultural perspective and creative imagination. As a child, I loved the billowing incense during the Mass and sound of bells that made me imagine what heaven must be like. The Saints were my friends, real people, and often gritty characters who sought to be the most authentic human beings and managing to make it into that communion of the blessed. Jesus was real to me when I looked at the crucified Christ. I would wonder why he would die such a horrible death. Then the enlightenment of the incarnation and redemption came to me during catechism class. I grasped what was intuitively present in my familial values and beliefs. It became alive for me—a concrete, tangible experience of the Divine.

For Catholics, the physical world is viewed as the place where God makes his presence known to humanity. Andrew Greeley, in his book, *The Catholic Imagination,* draws the distinction between a Catholic world-view and a Protestant world-view. The Catholic view sees God present in the material universe, in human experience and the gritty everydayness of human existence.[1] It is an analogical view, as theologian David Tracy notes in his book *The Analogical Imagination*. He delineates how Catholics use analogy in order to arrive at knowledge of God, and so find God present in the material world.[2] Protestants tend to view God as absent from the world yet known through dramatic moments of revelation such as the incarnation and redemption of humanity through Christ's passion and death. This is a dialectical imagination.[3] God is seen as other. Richard Blake, in *AfterImage*, quotes Richard McBrien who distinguishes these two approaches. He says that the dialectical perspective means that there is opposition between *for* and *against*. The analogical imagination sees realities as having more similarities than differences.[4] Catholics view life as communal and Protestants tend to emphasize the individual. Both of these are extreme tendencies and rarely are absolute in anyone. It gives us a way of understanding how Catholic filmmakers, whether they are practicing Catholics or not, view the world through their imaginations that have been conditioned by their early lives' experience of sacramentality, mediation, and communion.[5] These three elements are what make a Catholic imagination.

Sacramentality

Sacramentality is about "seeing God in all things" which Ignatius of Loyola posed to the Jesuits as a spiritual vision. When we are attuned to God's presence in the everydayness, in the ups and downs of life, in the messiness of relationships, then we are more apt to have a positive, hopeful outlook on life. Not that everything goes perfectly well and life has a fairy tale ending. Instead, life has

1. Greeley, *Catholic Imagination*, 5.
2. Tracy, *Analogical Imagination*, 446.
3. Blake, *AfterImage*, 8.
4. Ibid., 8.
5. Ibid., 13–14.

61

meaning and purpose. This is not the end, no matter how hard our post postmodern nihilist society tries to tell us otherwise. The Catholic imagination keeps alive the hope of life beyond death. This world is not all there is. We know it. Life beyond death is ingrained in us. It oozes from our pores and rattles our consciences. This is seen perhaps most clearly in Martin Scorsese's films. He is not a theologian and so he may misinterpret points of the Church's doctrine and even confuse matters of belief. Still, he is a man searching for meaning and hope amid the suffering. His characters, as dark and morally confused as they seem, are really microcosms of the conscience of the world. The desire for *something more* always lurks beneath the surface. It is the longing for the supernatural, for something beyond what this world alone can offer, the hope for happiness and peace, the hungering for intimacy, communion, and connection.

Scorsese's crime thriller *The Departed* reflects this human need for redemption, even with desperate and gnawing consciences. The title itself is based on a Catholic concept of "the faithful departed," those who have died in Christ's peace. Some may wonder with all the seemingly gratuitous violence in the film, how can it portray the Catholic imagination? Catholicism is all about the drama: the sacrifice of Christ on the cross that is renewed in every Eucharistic Liturgy. It is also depicted in the iconic Sacred Heart pictures of Jesus's bleeding heart that are present in several scenes of the film. It is through this bloody sacrifice that we are redeemed. Not only through the sacrifice, but also through the resurrection that destroys human sinfulness and restores humanity to a right relationship with God. It is in the sacramentality of a bloody sacrifice that life has meaning. The moral consequences to our actions symbolize the need for redemption.

The Departed, a good-cop-bad-cop narrative, structured around the Irish Catholic South Boston police department and the mob boss, Frank Costello (Jack Nicholson), is loosely based on the infamous mobster, Whitey Bulger. When two young cops, Colin Sullivan (Matt Damon) and William Costigan (Leonardo DiCaprio) go undercover in opposite ways, both the police and the mobsters discover a mole in their midst. The two undercover spies then scramble to try to uncover the other before they are found out. It is a story about crime and its moral consequences. As Scorsese says, this is a film that starts and ends at a "moral ground zero." It is about the choices we make and how those choices ✓ have specific outcomes. Matt Damon reflects by saying that the extreme violence is not gratuitous violence in the film because, "The characters all pay a price for the violence they inflict upon the others."[6] It is about sacrifice, but at what cost? Is it for another or for selfish gain, as it was for Damon's character, Colin? He liked the money Costello was dishing out to him to be the mole in the police department. In the end, however, it all comes to nothing. The religious dictum of the Gospel rings true, that what you have you cannot take with you when you die.

Another filmmaker for whose sense of sacramentality naturally presents itself in his art is Alejandro G. Iñárritu, the director who won back-to-back Best Director Oscars for *Birdman or (The Unexpected Virtue of Ignorance)* and *The Revenant*. Both have extensive symbolism and leave the viewer wondering what really happens to the main character and whether the point of the story was in the end an inherent intuition about the supernatural element of life. However, *The Revenant* will be our focus on how the terrible force of nature, untamed by human beings, can present powerful beauty that nurtures and sustains one lost in its fierce wilderness. It is a story inspired by true events in the life of Hugh Glass, a nineteenth-century legendary American West explorer who struggles for survival after a brutal bear attack when leading fur trappers through the Rocky Mountains along the Missouri River. The film fictionalizes the story for dramatic effect and includes Glass's (Leonardo DiCaprio) half-Pawnee Indian son, Hawk (Forrest Goodluck), who joins him in the expedition. After the bear attack, Major Henry (Domhnall Gleeson), leader of the party, offers money for two trappers to stay with Glass and his son in order to give him a proper burial. The ruthless John Fitzgerald (Tom Hardy) volunteers along with a teenager named Bridger

6. "Morality of 'The Departed.'"

63

(Will Poulter). After several days, Fitzgerald tries to suffocate Glass but is approached by Hawk whom Fitzgerald kills in view of Glass who is too weak to respond. Eventually he is abandoned for dead and thrown into a shallow grave. His will to survive and revenge his son's death and his own abandonment strengthens him to crawl two hundred miles to seek out Fitzgerald.

During Glass's quest for survival in the brutal winter wilderness he keeps recalling the voice of his deceased Pawnee wife who calls him to survive by saying, "As long as you still grab a breath, you fight." Throughout the film we hear Glass's struggle for breath, for life, for justice. His breath is symbolic of the Spirit breathing new life into those who are burdened by pain, sin, and injustice while also offering peace. Another powerful symbol is when Glass rides a horse off a cliff to escape the murderous Ree tribe. He survives by falling into a tree, which cradles him, and breaks his fall to the icy ground. When he comes to, he staves off hypothermia by crawling naked into the carcass of the fallen horse. It looks like a tomb from which he resurrects with new energy and drive. The scene that follows is of the sun bursting through the glass-like icicles on the trees causing them to melt and rain droplets onto him. It is as if beauty is melting away the violence of revenge in his heart. He still pursues his enemy but in the end lets Fitzgerald go to be dealt with by the powerful Ree. Revenge only creates a cycle of violence. As Iñárritu expresses, revenge is "an unwholesome emotion."[7] He continues, "What is after revenge? It leaves you empty" and it does not bring back what you have lost. The story, according to him, is about how to transform pain, and that "violence has huge consequences."[8] Forgiveness can be the only freeing response, the only way to truly find life.

7. McCracken, "Alejandro Gonzalez Iñárritu," 2, lines 2–3.
8. Ibid.

Mediation

The second characteristic of the Catholic imagination is mediation. For a Catholic, the created world reveals God's presence and spe- ✓ cific people and objects function as mediators for God in the world. People become instruments through which God's grace transforms another's life. We see this clearly in the film *Gimme Shelter* directed by Ronald Krauss, based on the story of an incredibly inspiring woman, Kathy DiFiore who once was homeless, turned her life around, and now runs Several Sources Shelters to help homeless pregnant mothers. The story is centered on Apple (Vanessa Hudgens), a troubled teen of a drug-abusing mother June (Rosario Dawson) who turns to the streets, then to her absent father Tom (Brendan Fraser) who forces her to have an abortion. After she flees from the abortion clinic she crashes a car landing up in the hospital. Through the gentle spiritual guidance of Father McCarthy (James Earl Jones), she goes to this shelter for pregnant teens. Life for this young girl is mediated through the directors of the shelter, the priest who led her there for assistance, and through the other homeless young women. Her life begins to have meaning. She finds hope and new life especially through the birth of her child. God very often works through other people for our good.

Another example of mediation in the Catholic imagination are the films comprising *The Decalogue,* directed by Krzysztof Kieslowski, a Polish cultural Catholic who professes to be an atheist even though he is concerned with the transcendent. He seeks *the more* in many of his narratives. In *The Decalogue,* which deals with moral issues based on the Ten Commandments, Kieslowski struggles with the issues of God and belief through avoidance or lightly touching on the topics. His Catholicism, however, has not left his imagination. This idea of mediation is present in many of the films comprising *The Decalogue.* In the first film, Krzysztof (Henryk Baranowski), an atheist and professor enthralled with science, teaches his son Paweł (Wojciech Klata) the very humanist ✓ doctrine that we ourselves can find the answers to life's problems. Yet, Krzysztof's sister, Irena (Maja Komorowska), who helps raise the child, is a devout Catholic and she teaches Paweł his catechism. When tragedy strikes the father blames himself and rushes into a church. It is there where redemption happens. No answers are given but somehow through the mediation of the faith of others the father feels a connection to the supernatural, to faith in a God who is more present to us than we are to ourselves.

Mel Gibson's film *Hacksaw Ridge* masterfully tells the true story of Desmond Doss (Andrew Garfield), a religious conscientious objector who enlists in the Army during World War II. He believes he can enter the military as a medic and so not use a weapon in battle. After much emotional and verbal abuse he is allowed to remain in the Army, however, ridiculed and shunned by fellow soldiers and officers. During a heated battle in Okinawa, the Allies are forced off a ridge in retreat after suffering extensive casualties. Doss alone remains on the ridge rescuing the wounded by dragging them under fire to the ridge's edge and lowering them down on a rope. All the while he prays to God saying, "Just one more. Give me strength for just one more." Smitty (Luke Bracey), the first to call Doss a coward, lies in a foxhole severely wounded up on the ridge, when Doss jumps in for the night. He shares with Smitty that his aversion to firearms is a result of his nearly shooting his drunken father who pointed a gun at his mother. That experience so devastated him that he chose never to hold a gun again. His tenacity in saving others at the risk of his own safety, proved his courage. Through Doss's self-giving love, the wounded of both sides found life. They survived because of his godly centeredness in the midst of the horror of war. This is mediation at its pinnacle.

Communion

Communion is the third characteristic of the Catholic imagination. As Catholics we realize that we are redeemed as a community. We are individuals on our journeys of life and the need for community is what grounds us. It is because Catholicism expresses its beliefs through communal worship, a sharing of the Body and

Blood of Christ together as his body the Church, that communion is part of the Catholic imagination.

In the movie *Wild,* directed by Canadian Jean-Marc Vallee, Cheryl Strayed (Reese Witherspoon) lives a dissolute life of marital infidelity and drug addiction. After her mother's death, she struggles to get her life in order. She remembers what her mother told her, "You can put yourself in the way of beauty." It is then that she decides to hike 1,100 miles alone on the Pacific Crest trail from California to Oregon. Through the pain, struggle, emotion, and blisters Cheryl faces her loneliness in the solitude of the wilderness. She finds herself. It is not through her own powers that she survives the trek but through the other people she meets along the way and through the family she eventually has after this experience. We must make our own journeys in life and face our own demons, but in the end, we all need other people to make life livable and joyful while growing in wisdom and understanding. That need for others, the sense of communion molds the Catholic cinematic imagination. Cheryl forgives herself and that forgiveness opens her up to see the grace that is all around her—in nature, in beauty, in relationships.

The British filmmaker with Irish roots, John Michael McDonagh, a philosophical humanist, offers a view of humanity in need of connection and communion through his films. In *Calvary,* he presents the senior priest of the village, Father James Lavelle (Brendan Gleeson), as one who possesses a moral core. From the very beginning of the film he faces the dilemma in the confessional of a person who says they want to kill him for the past sins of a parishioner who abused him as a child and the church's supposed lack of response to the crime. The priest then lives out the week going about his pastoral duties as "shepherd of souls" while he solitarily wrestles over this dilemma with his conscience. McDonagh says that it is a story about human beings, and, he reflects that the film, "does end for me on a moment of grace" a "modicum of hope."[9] What this film offers is the realization that we need other people; we need community. Even though Father James lives through the

9. Robinson, "*Calvary*'s writer-director."

week without telling anyone else about his death threat, he, in his gruff humanness, seeks to bring his congregation of cynical lapsed Catholics back to their faith. His love for his community is what gives him strength in a moment of testing.

With all the Catholic imagery, such as confessionals where we seek forgiveness of God for our sinfulness, the Eucharist as a sign of communion with God and others, pictures of Mary and the saints that offer us inspiration along our journeys, McDonagh, whether knowingly or unknowingly, offers a Catholic worldview showing that redemption is possible, forgiveness is real, connection and communion are necessary. He provides images of his Catholic imagination for the world to grasp the deeper meaning present in the film, something that Catholics and non-Catholics alike will understand. *Calvary* is perhaps one of the most Catholic films of the century because of this. What does giving your life really mean? Father James, through his own brokenness, shows us most clearly.

Encountering Grace

It is in the analogy of the material world that we grasp a glimpse of the Divine. Religious imagination is grounding for those who use art to communicate what it truly means to be human. Whether filmmakers are aware of this or not is irrelevant. What matters is that through the material we encounter grace. Through the mediation of other people, events, and circumstances we discover the existential yearnings of humanity for what is beyond this world. In the experience of connection and communion with others, grace takes root and transforms us into authentic human beings. Film is an especially dynamic medium for expressing these profound truths. For, this vision of sacramentality, mediation, and communion makes for a truly Catholic imagination.

PART 3

Theology of Pop Music

8

Pop Music's Idols
and the One God

S INCE THE DAWN OF pop music in the 1950s with the birth of
rock 'n' roll, the music celebrity industry has developed into
a culture that reinforces the idolizing of its most famous or infamous characters. Pop music icons are entertainers, urged on by a
multi-billion dollar industry, where the music can sometimes play
a secondary role to the larger-than-life image the artist has created
of themselves or the music industry has made of them. Our American, celebrity-infatuated culture can give us pause to consider how
our monotheistic belief is understood in the popular culture that
often idolizes iconic status and how the worship of the One God
offers the culture what it most deeply seeks and desires.

Doctrine of God

What does worship of God, the Omnipotent One and Father of all
of creation mean for our contemporary world that often seeks immortal fame? Pope Benedict XVI writes that we cannot look at the
existence of God in a purely theoretical way but, in a practical sense,
realize that without God nothing would exist, since he is Being itself. * *em ?*
If God is only theory than we live perverse lives. He says ignorance
of God is equivalent to being enslaved to the "elemental principles of
this world" which is a type of worship that leads to slavery because

it is based on untruth.[1] For God alone is the omnipotent and omniscient Creator who has the power, "to call into being from non-being, from nothingness"[2] all that he creates.

The book of Exodus gives us greater insight into God when God reveals his name to Moses. This revelation, says Pope Benedict, changes how we understand God, since it is not a concept of God that is revealed, but a relationship. This effects how human beings understand themselves, the world, and the Divine.[3] This revelation of a relationship puts the world and human beings into the proper order of creation. If we look at creation from a mythological view, then the divine is the highest order within the created universe, so the gods of ancient Rome or Greece, for example, were considered the highest beings, then the world itself, human beings, and the rest of nature. But, with the revelation of God's name in Exodus, God is not only the highest being in the universe, but Being Itself—uncreated, unmediated. By saying to Moses, "I AM" (Exod 3:14), God transcends all of the cosmos and the created world, but is not separated from it. God initiates a relationship of love and communion with all of creation, especially with human beings.

Belief Leads to Freedom

Belief in God is to be in touch with the core of our being, for God does not live disconnected from us but, as Pope Benedict says, he is the very, "ground of our being"[4] and makes his presence felt at the core of our existence. We have difficulty knowing and believing in God, he says, because we so often live away from the center of our being, where God lives and speaks to us.[5] Since human beings do not always live at their core, we tend to move away from God who dwells there and seek outward for that which can

1. Benedict XVI, *Credo for Today*, 21.
2. John Paul II, *God, Father and Creator*, 135.
3. Benedict XVI, *Credo for Today*, 21.
4. Ibid., 22.
5. Ibid.

fulfill the existential desire. Belief in God reveals the very essence and purpose of objective reality. To separate belief in God from objective truth is to fail to recognize the essence of what religion is all about.[6]

As God is the very ground of our being, to really believe means to make a change, a profound shift of our being[7] in order to recognize God at our very core. For the Israelites, to shift from a polytheistic culture to belief in One God was to let go of the gods of one's own making, the gods of one's own possessions, and the renunciation of fear of the mysterious which is tamed by the worship of it.[8] He continues by saying that to give worship and assent to the One God, Father Almighty is to acknowledge the power that sustains and creates everything in the universe. To give over oneself to God is to accept that this power is not in humanity's grasp, nor is the divine himself.[9]

True belief in God means that we shift our focus of worship away from the locus of social power, pleasure, and the cult of fear[10] and instead redirect it toward the One who embraces all of humanity as a loving, tender Father. Belief in God is a renunciation of the gods of "power, bread, and Eros,"[11] which try to claim absoluteness over humanity. But, God, as the loving creator and Father-provider, has lavished upon humanity the, "superabundance of his love and has thus made good in advance all our deficiency."[12] God, a Person, is, "the objective ground of all reality,"[13] and so we can entrust ourselves to this Absolute with utter confidence since he is the Person who speaks to us and lives within us at the very core of our being. This is not oppression, but rather true freedom since it is a relationship of love. Therefore, "acceptance of the truth of the

---

6. Ibid., 24.

7. Ratzinger, *Introduction to Christianity*, 55.

8. Ibid., 74.

9. Ibid.

10. Ibid.

11. Ibid., 76.

12. Benedict XVI, *Credo for Today*, 12.

13. Ibid., 30.

Creator in his creatures, is worship."[14] Pope Benedict affirms that, this is why we can say: I believe in One God, Father Almighty, Creator of heaven and earth.

Icons Versus Idol

If God is One, Father and Creator, then how do we understand icons and iconography or the contemporary use of the term idol? Icons are images that signify the divine. Traditionally, in Christianity, icons are not of themselves worshipped, but only represent by image the One to whom we alone offer our worship and adoration. The commonly understood definition of idol is a false god or the worship of a representation or image of a god. This distinction is clear in theological and biblical terms, but in the contemporary use of language it often becomes muddled and the terms idol and icon are used interchangeably. Do contemporary Americans *worship* popular music celebrities? Are they simply icons representing and signifying some deeper desires or needs in humanity?

Pop Music Icons

To become a popular music icon one has to achieve a certain level of international fame and recognition, financial gain, and a long-term career that proves enduring to the public. Usually they are known by a single name, which is often reserved for religious figures: Jesus, Moses, Buddha, and Mohammed.[15] Some single-named pop icons are: Elvis, Sting, Whitney, Madonna, Prince, Tina, Ozzy, Beyoncé, Kesha, Nelly, Kanye, Pink, etc. These stars mix reality with fantasy to create an image of themselves for the public since the musical performance itself has made them into fictitious characters. Rupert Till, in his book, *Pop Cult: Religion and Popular Music,* goes on to explain that the superstar convinces the audience that what they are performing is their true self

14. Ibid., 31.
15. Till, *Pop Cult*, 47–49.

with all their authentic emotions, but in reality, they are storytelling. This is theater, and he says, "in this case quite literally all the world's a stage."[16]

Media Technologies and the Music Industry

In the popular music scene, those artists who have achieved iconic status have become larger-than-life figures with the development of television and current media technologies. Their faces are always before us and through cleverly concocted mediaphemes[17] they have become household icons. They are like gods, just like religious icons, projected on large screens, on billboards and posters, on our digital mobile screens, but the pop icons have the media technology that creates them as three-dimensional figures. Not only do they have their musical talent, but they also have videos, social media personas, action figures, and endless merchandise connected with them, all created by public relations companies that promote this imaginary person.[18] These pop icons have obtained that *divine status* of single name recognition and legendary image. Till says that this is what distinguishes the icon from the star.[19] Yet, is this what these artists desire to be, or is it the money-driven music industry that creates these artists into little gods? Often these artists can be manipulated by the "music machine" the business of technology that drives it. One music critic writes, "We worship at the altar of the technology that connects us with the music we choose to listen to."[20]

Some pop icons are true visionaries in the field of musical entertainment to the point that no one after them has yet seemed original enough to surpass their astounding creativity. Even

16. Ibid., 51.

17. See ibid., 49. *Mediaphemes* are media constructions that allow an artist to become a popular icon.

18. Ibid., 51.

19. Ibid., 48.

20. Catalano, "Where Have All the Rock Stars Gone?" lines 128–29.

though Michael Jackson, whom Elizabeth Taylor dubbed the "King of Pop," claimed the largest fan base ever while alive, he is still one of the highest-earning celebrities even after his death. He grosses more than two hundred million dollars a year on the sales of his music, shares in Sony, and the extensive merchandise connected to his iconic figure, which is only surpassed recently by U2. With all his issues of grandiosity, even having a fifteen-foot Michael statue erected in the Netherlands that was used during his 1995 *History* Tour, he is most admired as an entertainer *par excellence*. Many contemporary pop music icons borrow from Michael's innovative style: Flo Rida, Lady Gaga, Usher, Jay-Z, Justin Timberlake, and Bruno Mars. His cult celebrity status remains as the top pop music artist of all time. He often was criticized for pointing out the flaws of the industry that made him a star.

It is musical creativity that leads these artists into the industry. Sometimes, however, the industry crushes them to be made into an image other than who they really are. Perhaps this issue is not that the person themselves wants iconic status, but that they simply want to explore and share their craft. Lauryn Hill, a brilliant hip-hop artist from New Jersey abruptly left the industry in the 1990s at the supposed height of her career. She tells her story in an open letter widely publicized on music Internet sites criticizing the music industry as being exploitative, dysfunctional, and compromising. She calls it, "pop culture cannibalism." The marketing and politics of the industry sometimes prevents artists from exercising their full power and knowing their ability as artists. Lauryn found that she needed to pull away from that lifestyle that was requiring her to compromise her talents and detoxify herself from privileges and indulgences that she says come, "at the expense of my free soul, free mind, and therefore my health and integrity." Perhaps the system is to blame for creating the culture's deified icons and not the celebrities themselves who are mostly artists with tremendous talents and intense desires to share their gifts.

Lauryn is not alone in this struggle. Kelly Clarkson, too, after being named the first *American Idol* from the television show, eventually pulled away from the Sony music machine to branch out on her own and successfully explore the music she wanted to sing and perform. Numerous movies about iconic musical artists also tell of their personal struggles because of their fame, but also how the industry treated them. Movies such as *Ray* that portrays the turbulent career of Ray Charles, or *Walk the Line* about Johnny Cash who struggled with addiction but also the expectations of music moguls. *Dreamgirls,* though fictitious, tells of the talented singers who become caught up in the sweep of fame and privilege that they lose a sense of their personal musical integrity. Effie, powerfully played by Jennifer Hudson, another *American Idol* contestant, comes to find the music within herself she was always meant to sing. Eminem, often criticizing the "system" that brought him fame, explains his angst in the movie *8-Mile.*

Popular music stars can reach this iconic status much more so than film stars. This is so because film stars are seen occasionally in movies and act as different characters each time. Music artists, however, are living their image continuously *live* through their musical performances, concerts, and television appearances. They rarely turn off their iconic status, the image they have created or that was created for them—their mediapheme. American culture thrives on the consumption of popular icons through consumerism and commercialization. Through this market-driven industry, fans of the musical artist maintain the star's popularity as long as they buy their product. "This makes the maintenance of an obsessive devotion to the popular icon by the fan, a key relationship within popular music."[21] If this relationship is sustained then the icon's career continues. So, really, the musical talent of an artist is one small part of that artist's ability to be a star as is often expressed by the celebrity judges on *The Voice.* To become a pop star requires heart, self-expression, emotion, personality, and uniqueness. This popular music scene, then, is what drives the personality cults of these pop icons.

One of the most successfully creative television innovations is the development of the interactive reality singing competitions, *American Idol* and *The Voice.* Since *Idol*'s premier in 2002 it has

21. Till, *Pop Cult,* 52.

spawned numerous other reality TV music and dance competitions and impacted the history of television as a cultural phenomenon. While searching for the next pop music icon it cleverly uses television as free advertising and instant market research. The very name of the show suggests that people will latch onto a particular contestant and idolize their talent and star quality. Simon Fuller, the creator of *American Idol*, says, "Pop music is about celebrity and not just about music . . . . Pop stars should be icons."[22]

Search for Meaning

Fans see themselves in the stars they idolize. Often they are icons concocted from the hollow mediated images. Traditionally, religious icons are hallowed places or images that are inhabited by the Divine. The popular icon, on the other hand, is also hallowed, but the viewers or fans inhabit them. This means that, "the fans inhabit the place traditionally filled by a god, deifying themselves."[23] Music is always reflecting society's search for deeper meaning and transcendence[24] and so the fascination with popular music icons can be a sign of that quest for an understanding of the supernatural existential. Humanity seeks the divine. Human beings are always in search of God, the One who is *the* Creator and Sustainer of all life, the Father of humanity. We long for the love that only God, as loving and tender Father, can give.

Considering the needs that are supposedly fulfilled in celebrity adulation, the question of belief is brought to the fore. Is there a loss of God in today's popular culture as the ground of our being and the core of all objective reality? The cult of celebrity is obviously expressing people's need for worship, and is showing that a lack of belief in God leads people to accept lesser gods—finite, weak, and irrational fantasies of our media imaginations. The cult of celebrity expresses a deep longing in humanity for the divine. Our theological dialogue

22. Ibid., 100.
23. Ibid., 52.
24. Detweiler and Taylor, *Matrix of Meanings*, 132.

can speak to the narratives of a celebrity music culture that is full of symbols and metaphors. The search for what it means to be human is a constant theme in popular music and can be the opening for a discussion about our ultimate end and the desire for the supernatural that is innate in all human beings.

Sometimes human being's lack of awareness of God leads them to seek connection and fulfillment in something that is utterly beyond reality to a fictional iconic image from which they wish to be filled. What can Christians give as a witness to this culture of celebrity? Love. Pope Benedict says that the very ground of our being is a relationship, something more than I am to myself because, he says, "I can know only because I am known, love only because I am already loved."[25] It is about the, "finding of a 'thou' who gives me meaning, to whom I can entrust myself absolutely."[26] When we say, *I Believe*, we are saying a prayer since we are because God is, we can give of ourselves absolutely for he is absolute.[27]

---

25. Benedict XVI, *Credo for Today,* 29.

26. Ibid., 30.

27. Ibid.

9

The Existential Soul of Pop Music

P EOPLE WHO KNOW ME know that I am a pop music junkie. I enjoy hearing a familiar retro song that brings me back to my teenage years and the memories that evokes. But I especially revel in listening to the creative new talents and songs that top the Billboard charts weekly, scanning all the genres of pop, hip-hop, R&B, country, and rock. Music speaks to me like no other medium. Coming from a family of dancers is perhaps why music touches me deeply in both body and soul. It opens up my soul articulating my existential desires and struggles. Music, like the Psalms in the Scriptures, gives expression to people's feelings and yearnings. As Chance the Rapper says in his song "Blessings," the challenges of life present the opportunity to praise God even amid the suffering. The pop songs that fill our playlists are the psalms of today.

Music is one of the most powerful influences on human beings. It affects us at an emotional level deep within the soul communicating our thoughts and emotions. Innumerable styles of music and genres from all parts of the world flood the airways. Every nationality has music at its cultural core that defines a people with their joys and sorrows, hopes and fears, elations and frustrations. Music, like no other medium, creates community and dispels differences, uniting people together.

The music I reference here is popular music that is the mainstream music *of the people* from the 1950s onward when it became associated with youth culture, making it *popular*. What is it about pop music that moves us to tears and laughter? Why do fans become enthralled with their favorite artists? Popular music begins and ends with personal experience, especially during our youth. We all remember the songs of our youth, we know all the lyrics, and still have an emotional connection to them. That connects us to people of the same generation when at parties, old pop songs are sung by the whole crowd. We also go to pop music to find comfort, solace, and meaning for our lives. It is a place for self-expression, individually and communally, and can be a reflection of the spiritual.

Music as Expression

Since music enhances feelings, young people use music as a form of self-expression to give voice to their emotions and moods. Most youth listen to over five hours of music a day, so the importance of music to a youth culture cannot be underestimated. Their music tells others who and what gives formulation to their personal identity. A person's playlist tells a lot about who they are and what they most desire.

Music has the power to bring people together. Consider any pop music or rock concert. There is a spiritual connection with the others in attendance. We relate through the music as a socializing event. We also listen to music individually, especially with the invention of the Sony Walkman and then later with MP3 players and iPods, and now through every digital mobile device and streaming service. We immerse ourselves in our music since it expresses something deep inside of us and speaks to the heart. David Grohl, frontman for the Foo Fighters, stated once at the Grammys that, "the human element of making music is the most important." He continues, "Singing into a microphone and learning to play an instrument and learning to do your craft, that's the most important thing for people to do. It's not about being perfect, it's not about

81

sounding absolutely correct, it's not about what goes on in a computer. It's about what goes on in here [pointing to his heart] and what goes on in here [pointing to his head]."

Music Is Spiritual

LL Cool J, while hosting the Grammys, was not the first person to say that music is profoundly spiritual. Augustine wrote that music is the science that leads most to theology.[1] It transforms and leads us from the temporal world to the eternal. Music leads one to God, says Augustine. Boethius follows up on Augustine's thoughts and writes that music has the power to affect one's soul, to reach to the depths of the person where they are truly themselves and where they meet God, the Creator.[2] Many pop songs have spiritual overtones and references because they speak about the human condition that is the starting point for grace to work. These songs offer us a glimpse into theology, as Augustine would say.

Theology and Pop Music

Craig Detweiler and Barry Taylor, in their book, *A Matrix of Meanings: Finding God in Pop Culture,* state that we can speak of God and popular culture because of, "the creative nature of God and faith."[3] Our sacramental imagination comes into play here as well. The use of language, poetry, symbols, sounds, and emotions in popular music reflect God's creative presence in the world. Pharrell Williams's song "Happy" is so infectious with its rhythmic sounds and upbeat tempo that one feels happy just listening to it. Hundreds of thousands of YouTube videos of people who sing and dance to this song flood the Internet. The lyrics symbolize our transcendent desires for what space and time cannot limit, the desire for happiness that is infinite. Multi-platinum Grammy

1. Quoting Augustine in Millbank, *Radical Orthodoxy,* 243.
2. Ibid.
3. Detweiler and Taylor, *Matrix of Meanings,* 151.

winning artist, Taylor Swift's song "Look What You Made Me Do" reflects back to her fans and all those who doubted her artistry that nothing holds her back. She sells more records than any music artist. It may seem defiant, but in light of her legal issues against sexual misconduct in the industry, she gives women a voice to help end the silent tyranny of exploitation and expresses her boldness to do what is right. Grammy winner Sam Smith hit the charts with his soulful ballad, "Stay With Me," singing about the need for someone to be with us along our journey of life. "Something Just Like This" by The Chainsmokers and Coldplay defy the superhero myth that the one person we want to spend our lives with has to have superhuman powers. Instead, they sing of being with a person who is there for them, a companion, someone who simply is. The sacramental experience of touch represents communion with another and a way to alleviate our lonesomeness. We are created for communion.

Sometimes it is popular music that helps us to articulate the difficult issues of life, as in Linkin Park's song, "What I've Done," which reflects on the destructive actions human beings have wrought on the planet. The song seeks forgiveness for all of humanity. Popular music often deals with the angst of life, the pain and suffering, just as theology. Yelawolf along with Eminem express this in the song "Best Friend." The lyrical refrain tells of when one feels oppressed by others only God offers complete acceptance. Then in classic Eminem style, the rapper expounds upon how those who judge others will be judged by God and those abused will be justified before God. Our darkest emotions are not difficult for God. The Psalms exemplify the gamut of human emotions, including anger, frustration, and bitterness. All can be sacramental moments in our lives if we look to their deeper meaning and the grace that God offers in the midst of our everydayness. Kesha's song "Praying" expresses her deep pain in overcoming abuse and her peace while offering forgiveness to those who wronged her.

Music is art and art is an expression of the soul. The soul, being non-material, constantly searches, seeking for something more. So many music artists are seekers, though sometimes misguided. They look for meaning, an end to an oppressive way of life that comes from poverty, violence, and shattered relationships, prevalent in many urban settings. The movie *8-Mile* by and about Eminem portrays this quest, as well as *Straight Outta Compton* about the legendary gansta hip-hop group N.W.A. Their controversial lyrics spoke about what they saw as law enforcement prejudice and a drug-infested lifestyle of the streets.

Tupac Shakur, a tremendous poet who died at age twenty-five, penned an insightful poem about pain, suffering, and the hope of something more to come. A gansta rapper who lived through hellish situations, he possessed a depth of spirituality that astounds both fans and critics alike. His poem, "The Rose that grew from the cement" stirs the soul with its powerful emotions communicating how one rises from the ashes of oppression and economic deprivation. Bono and his group U2, while not promoters of organized religion, sing about many explicitly spiritual topics. Their album *Songs of Innocence* provides a musical sweep of their lives and moments of grace, such as in the song "Iris (Hold Me Close)" that was written for Bono's mother who died when he was young. In it he addresses his sorrow through music, thereby healing the memories while experiencing grace. U2's songs are often lines lifted right from Scripture, creating a modern book of Psalms full of emotional outbursts that seeks answers from God to ease the pain in the world.

Chance the Rapper's album *Coloring Book*, the first streaming-only collection to win a Grammy, affords a glimpse into his soul. It developed after his short stint in Hollywood went awry and he moved back to his hometown of Chicago connecting with a former girlfriend. They have a baby girl born with an atrial flutter. This experience forces him to focus his life on his family. His album speaks deeply to his religious roots but also to his increasingly mature understanding of life. In an interview on Beats 1 Radio with Zane Lowe he confesses, "I think the new generation and the forward is all about freedom and all about the ability to do what we want. We're not free unless we can talk about God." Lowe then comments, "There's no mystery that faith in music and faith in God go hand-in-hand a lot of times."[4]

So much of pop music deals with the angst of being human, ✓ as does our faith. Music addresses the anger and frustration of those who are economically depressed. Rap and hip-hop come from this place, but rock music sometimes does as well. Bob Seger and Bruce Springsteen sing about the despair of unemployment of the white working class, the struggles of veterans returning from war, and the disturbing political shortsightedness that perpetrates such situations. Through all this, God is present in the culture, in its torturous pain and suffering. As Detweiler and Taylor suggest, it is precisely there in the popular culture where Jesus, the Man of Sorrows, is found.[5]

True Freedom

In our study of theology, we listen to the aspirations, concerns, and struggles that music of the popular culture expresses and respond to it with the message of the Gospel. Popular culture seeks a savior and a redeemer thereby generating the need to create icons, idolizing those who have what many aspire to possess. Fame is the goal of the popular culture. It is after all about being *popular*. People look for recognition as well as remembrance. So much about the celebrity-obsessed culture revolves around status—who is in and who is out. Pop music idols' mantra centers on freedom. They want to be free to express who they are or who they have created their mediaphemes to be, that is, their media construct which enables them to achieve pop star status and be revered as an icon.[6] However, what is true freedom? Is it simply choices without rules or guides? Theology offers a much deeper reflection on authentic freedom that moves outside the orbit of the self.

4. Sarachik, "Chance the Rapper," line 28–29.
5. Detweiler, *Matrix of Meanings*, 152.
6. Till, *Pop Cult*, 49.

Freedom is not merely the capacity for choice between objects. It exists only because there is transcendence and the starting point is God. God is present in every act of human freedom, by the very nature of freedom itself, as Karl Rahner would say.[7] This references not merely freedom of acts, but reaches to the heart of the person, "the permanent constitutive of man's nature,"[8] It is about freedom for our final end—salvation or damnation, a "freedom of being," namely, "a transcendental mark of human existence itself."[9] This involves the ability to say yes or no to oneself. True freedom, then, begins with self-mastery that can be a self-realization either for a relationship with God or a refusal of God.

A theological view of freedom understands it as a gift of the heart, a capacity for love. The more free one is the more one can let go and live in *kenosis*, a self-emptying embrace of life. To our contemporary culture this may seem absurd. Many rappers sing about getting as much out of life as possible, to the point of a hoarding hedonism. This often comes out of an oppressive economic situation that spawns the opposite reaction. However, it generates enslavement to that part of being human that seeks to *be* God rather than *for* God. Recognizing our place in the order of creation cultivates self-mastery and selflessness. Hans Urs von Balthasar says that, "God remains the center, and man is drawn beyond himself toward the absolute as it manifests itself. He 'possesses' love only insofar as love possesses him."[10] The more one is truly free the more one relates to others in love. The pop music culture sees a freedom without any restraint, a freedom from hindrance to do as one pleases. It is a self-centered and individualistic view of freedom that engages a philosophy of self-determining indulgence. The Christian view, on the other hand, produces a giving oneself in love that allows one to be true to the very core of one's being, one's essence. Rahner writes, "Love alone allows man

7. Rahner, *Theological Investigations*, Vol. 6, 180.

8. Ibid., 181.

9. Ibid., 184.

10. von Balthasar, *Love Alone is Credible*, 134.

to forget himself."[11] Human beings do not create themselves or determine their beginning and end. The only true act of freedom subsists in freedom of being that is selfless and self-surrendering. True freedom demands self-sacrifice, to "lay down one's life for one's friends" (John 15:13). This sense of freedom is how cultural mystics can challenge the popular music culture's artists to reflect the power and dignity of true human love and freedom.

Music as Language of the Body

The body is sacred and we experience God through our emotions and senses. God's gift generates the incarnational experience of the supernatural in the natural, the divine in the human. Jesus fully realized this being the Son of God Incarnate. Every human being is both body and soul, human and divine, natural and supernatural. We long for that connection to God, our Creator and Redeemer, and we express it in our body through worship and adoration. We are rational creatures with the ability to reason right from wrong, understand our passions, and choose to act responsibly respecting both others and ourselves. Our body communicates that incarnational experience.

Simon Frith, in his book, *Performing Rites*, points out that in listening to pop music we are, "listening to a performance."[12] Listening, he says, is in fact a performance. Watching and listening to a music artist perform is an experience of a persona which they have assumed. There are numerous music artists who epitomize performance in order to give meaning to the songs they sing. Nicki Minaj and Katy Perry, through their lyric and showmanship, offer the public a mask of who they are underneath all the makeup and costuming. A question we can raise: How much of their stage or video performance of a song presents a separate cultural meaning than the song itself?

11. Rahner, *Theological Investigations*, Vol. 6, 187.

12. Frith, *Performing Rites*, 203.

The artist performs a narrative, says Frith, and gives meaning through the visuals. The artist herself is a medium for giving meaning. He says, "performance art is a form of rhetoric," which allows the artist to tell a story.[13] Does this take away from the art of the medium of the music itself or does it layer it by giving it multiple meanings? The role of the audience then is to interpret it through their own experience. Frith quotes Richard Baumann who says that performance is, "'an emergent structure'; it comes into being only as it is being performed."[14] The performer and the audience interpret the story at the same time. The audience listens to the music and the performance with all its visual, sensual elements. And the performer tells the viewers what they think of their own music by their very movements to it.[15]

Performance can be spiritual, but the body has a theological meaning of itself that begs our attention especially with regard to the sensuality in which pop music revolves. Detweiler and Taylor explain that music is holistic and involves both body and soul, just as our faith does,[16] which can offer a sacred sensuality. However, can the performance also distract the viewer from a true understanding of the human body? Perhaps it revolves around how we see and understand the body in our relationship with God. Is there a theological examination that gives expression to the incarnational belief that God dwells within the human body? Pope John Paul II's revolutionary compilation, *Theology of the Body* proposes an answer.

13. Ibid., 205.

14. Ibid., 208.

15. Ibid., 224.

16. Detweiler and Taylor, *Matrix of Meanings*, 151.

10

Theology of the Body and Pop Music

CULTURAL MYSTICISM IS ABOUT a supernatural relationship rooted in our earthly reality. When we enter into a profound experience of God we are not miraculously removed from our material existence. That gnostic-like reasoning dichotomizes the human person whereas we are unified in our physical, spiritual, emotional, and sexual selves. A true mystic reflects holistically on the cultural experience in which the body, mind, and soul are engaged in this grace-filled encounter. This means that even in this highly sexualized culture God's truth can be revealed and lived.

Music and Sexuality

Most popular songs are about relationships and love. Music gives expression to the human experience, and one of the most powerful forces within the human person is sexuality, the desire of being united with another, the giving of oneself. Human beings experience the drive along with the euphoria and the consequences, the morality and the guilt. Sex triggers some of the most dramatically formidable emotions—elation, love, joy, ecstasy, as well as heartbreak, disappointment, and shame. It is often a topic addressed through those mediums that seek to explain the complexities of this powerful human experience, notably in popular music. We try to make sense of it through art, which by its nature begs to give expression to the inexpressible. But what does popular music say about the human person? What are human beings searching for through sexuality? How can a philosophy about the human person give meaning to a culture seeking true love and bliss?

Karol Wojtyla—actor, philosopher, professor, bishop, pope— pondered these questions for many years especially when he worked with the young people of his time who were searching for meaning in human relationships. His anthropological personalism gives direction for this search. He opens up a positive view of the human person and human sexuality that can bring joy and hope to human living. He starts with human experience[1] and the value and dignity of the human person. His philosophy eventually developed into a comprehensive *Theology of the Body*, which sees the human person as the place where God dwells and is present in humanity's search for fulfillment and intimacy.

The personalism of Karol Wojtyla references the person as the source of all that happens within.[2] His core philosophical premise is that by acting the human person is realized and becomes who he or she really is. The act of the person, which is *conscious action*, expresses the person as a being who acts in freedom and responsibility. Consciousness is the core of our acting and self-knowledge.[3] For him, "action serves as a particular moment of apprehending— that is, of experiencing—the person."[4] And so every true act of the human person is a moral act with moral value, either morally good or morally bad. For Wojtyla, awareness is crucial in this knowledge of oneself with moral responsibility.

In this act of self-knowledge, human beings obtain self-possession and self-governance, as well as self-determination.[5] This is the transcendence that is sought by the human spirit, the innate knowledge that is part of our being itself. Wojtyla reflects that the

1. Wojtyla, *Person and Community*, 188.
2. Wojtyla, *Acting Person*, 66.
3. Ibid., 20.
4. Ibid., 10.
5. Ibid., 106.

experience of the human person is one of a self-determining agent who is realized through one's free and responsible actions. Avery Dulles, in reflecting on Wojtyla's *The Acting Person* says that, "Activity is not something strictly other than the person; it is the person coming to expression and constituting itself."[6] In making choices between values or various options, the person determines himself and his value and so becomes, "his own primary object."[7] There is a constant seeking for completeness and self-fulfillment.

Love as Self-Fulfillment

In the world of popular music culture, this desire for self-fulfillment remains a determining agent expressing itself in the lyrics, rhythms, and rhymes of popular music, present in the music of such pop artists as: Imagine Dragons, Drake, Justin Bieber, Shawn Mendes, Ed Sheeran, Miley Cyrus, Coldplay, and The Script. Wojtyla affirms this search and this desire when he says, "The very fact that the self exhibits a tendency to realize itself is proof of its incompleteness."[8] Lady Gaga herself says in an interview with Ellen DeGeneres, that what she espouses, "is all about self-worship and self-fulfillment." Is this the true fulfillment Wojtyla speaks about?

In order to understand the view of the person as a self-fulfilling agent, the person who acts consciously toward self-determination and transcendence, we need to comprehend Wojtyla's understanding of freedom and love. For him, freedom is not only about the will choosing one option over another, but authentic freedom realizes being itself. As human beings our very nature is free and freedom compels a movement toward the other in love. Every act of the will is a response to values or objects, which are presented as good or an answer to self-transcendence and self-determination. However, as Avery Dulles comments, "The freedom of the human person is not to be understood indeterministically, as though it meant emancipation from all constraints. Although

6. Dulles, "John Paul II," 12.

7. Wojtyla, *Toward a Philosophy of Praxis*, 14.

8. Ibid.

the mind must conform to the real order, law as a moral obligation is not something merely mechanical or biological. It presupposes a subject with personal consciousness."[9] For Wojtyla and later as John Paul II, true and authentic freedom, "is never freedom 'from' the truth but always and only freedom 'in' the truth."[10]

Freedom that is self-fulfilling is never separated from self-giving love, according to Wojtyla's personalistic norm. Love is the true fulfillment of the person. How one loves others depends essentially upon the point when a person has discovered him or herself as worthy of love and how deeply he or she accepts that.[11] Wojtyla's personalistic norm presents both a negative and a positive perspective. He says, "The person is the kind of good which does not admit of use, and cannot be treated as an object of use and as such as the 'means to an end,'" and, "The person is a good toward which the only proper and adequate attitude is love."[12]

The True and the Good

Our actions as self-determining agents have a moral value. The morality of an act reveals the dignity of the human person.[13] If the act is morally good it actualizes the good, which the person essentially is. Determining the morality of an act is always based on a reference to truth, which Wojtyla explains. In every human action the person tends toward some perceived good, but not every action fulfills the full realization of the person. Fulfillment comes not through the act itself but through the moral goodness of the act.[14] His philosophical personalism, then, is based on the dignity of the human person, "the primacy of the person over things . . . . The

---

9. Dulles, "John Paul II," 17.

10. John Paul II, *Veritatis Splendor*, No. 64.

11. Szostek, "Karol Wojtyla's View," 59.

12. Wojtyla, *Love and Responsibility*, 41.

13. Ibid., 138–39.

14. Szostek, "Karol Wojtyla's View," 58.

sense of the transcendence of the human person over the world and of God over the human person."[15]

The moral goodness of an act is seen in reference to the truth and a dependence on truth.[16] If there is disloyalty to the truth that is when a person is enslaved. And without reference to the dignity of the human person there is moral immaturity.[17] This leads to utilitarianism—seeing the moral act for its usefulness for the person's own attainment of happiness without reference either to one's own dignity nor the dignity of others. Wojtyla's personalism responds to this utilitarian view by saying that a person is most fully him or herself when one is for others, that is, acts in giving of oneself out of love for another.[18]

The Body and Music

Popular music, as I have said, most often references relationships and sexuality. Flo Rida, in his song "Wild Ones," speaks of the sexual encounter, in reference to his personal pleasure, just as "Body Like a Back Road" by Sam Hunt. Simon Frith, in his book, *Performing Rites: On the Value of Popular Music*, suggests that it is "in what we bring *to* music rather than in what we find *in* it, that sexual suggestions lie."[19] So, is it in the language of the body referenced in popular music that creates sexual stimulation, or is it the social sensitivities that give the music and lyrics meaning? How is the body portrayed and does it respect the dignity of the human person?

Sexual references in popular music have been present since the dawn of rock n' roll in the 1950s. In fact, arias and operas from centuries past speak of this existential human drive. However, the explicitness of contemporary popular music's mention of sexual activity has increased with the growth of hip-hop music. Psychology professor Dawn Hobbs did a study that shows how 92

15. John Paul II, *Ex Corde Ecclesiae*, No. 18.

16. Szostek, "Karol Wojtyla's View," 57.

17. Ibid., 60.

18. Ibid.

19. Frith, *Performing Rites*, 143.

percent of songs on the billboard charts deal with sexuality.[20] This is no surprise. With all the expanse of human intelligence and its infinite pursuit for attainment of knowledge, this biological, psychological, emotional, and spiritual aspect of human sexuality still defies total human understanding. It is perhaps because it is an innate drive in the human soul for connection and intimacy. What human beings ultimately seek through sexual intimacy is supernatural, something that can never be satisfied with anything natural alone. Humanity is "wired" for the infinite, the supernatural, and the eternal.

During his pontificate, Pope John Paul II provides a systematic teaching of the meaning of masculinity, femininity, the body as gift, and the spousal meaning of the body in a relationship between man and woman, which he calls his *Theology of the Body*, a particular aspect of theological anthropology.[21] His starting point is the biblical Creation story in Genesis. He reflects on the origins of human beings: original solitude, original unity, and original nakedness. He saw the split in the philosophical thought prevalent in his day between the person and nature, a dualism that was promoted by scientific rationalism. He instead promotes the unity of man in his body,[22] the beauty of the body, and God's original intent for humanity.

This is "good news" for a culture that rejects the medieval theological response to sex as a necessary evil. In the 1950s, rock 'n' roll music artists challenged the puritanical views of human sexuality prevalent in American and European society at that time. There was Little Richard, Chuck Berry, Elvis Presley, Aretha Franklin, Muddy Waters, and Fats Domino. Then into the 1960s with The Beatles, Marvin Gaye, Jimi Hendrix and the rockers, Led Zepplin, The Doors, and The Rolling Stones adding their viewpoints. It continues in every decade with new artists who push the limits of social acceptability regarding sexuality. Today listening to Ne-Yo, Rhianna, Kendrick Lamar, Nicki Minaj, or Lil'

20. For a well-researched article on sexuality in the songs of top billboard charts, see Herbert, "Sex Sells."

21. John Paul II, *Man and Woman He Created Them*, 3:4.

22. John Paul II, *Letter to Families*, No. 19.

Wayne we hear language creating the feeling of sex along with the rhythms. Simon Frith says, "Music is 'sexy' not because it make us move, but because (through that movement) it makes us feel; make us feel (like sex itself) intensely present."[23] How does this experience of music reflect an image of the human body? Is it personalism as a respect for the body or utilitarianism through the use of someone else's body for my pleasure? Our theological understanding challenges the prevalent culture's philosophical concepts of the human person or its lack thereof. A human being cannot be relegated to a thing, but must be respected as a divine gift with all the dignity that entails.

Karol Wojtyla appreciated and affirmed humanity's creativity in the arts. Being an actor himself, he could appreciate the passionate sense of the human person proposed by artists in their genres. In his *Letter to Artists*, when he was Pope John Paul II, he wrote that this is why artists, "the more conscious they are of their 'gift,' are led all the more to see themselves and the whole of creation with eyes able to contemplate and give thanks, and to raise to God a hymn of praise. This is the only way for them to come to a full understanding of themselves, their vocation, and their mission."[24] The more fully human beings live the sense of their dignity and worth, the more they grow in truth, freedom, and love, and the more they will respect themselves, their bodies, and other human beings, seeing them not as objects of pleasure to be used but as unique and beautiful gifts of the Creator.

The Gift of Oneself

Christianity is not about a *what* but a *who*. We need not have an objectifying view of the human body but a subjective consciousness that respects each person as gift. John Paul II says that, "When one becomes a gift for others that one most fully becomes oneself."[25] No one is equal to one's body parts as sometimes it is suggested in

23. Frith, *Peforming Rites*, 144.
24. John Paul II, *Letter to Artists*, No. 1.
25. Wojtyla, *Person and Community*, 194.

the popular music culture. The person is not an item to be used as an object of pleasure. The person has existential worth and beauty that cannot be objectified but is to be respected and honored. Wojtyla's view affirms the pop music cultural icons of today who seek transcendence and fulfillment and challenges the use of the body solely for pleasure. Avery Dulles succinctly sums up Wojtyla's call: √ "We cannot fulfill ourselves except through transcending ourselves and giving ourselves in love toward others."[26] Wojtyla calls this the "law of the gift" and gives the anthropological grounding for the maxims of Jesus in the Gospels that say we must give in order to receive, die in order to live.[27]

Popular music gives expression to the deepest emotions of human experience and the artists sing about challenging issues of human living—the light and the dark. Wojtyla would applaud those artists who aid us in confronting our humanness and our sense of community. But, we cannot remain there. His anthropological personalism is the catalyst for the culture today to understand the human person more profoundly and its search for transcendence and meaning. Only by accepting the person as gift can we learn true love and happiness. Human beings are most fully themselves when they give themselves as gift and if reciprocated it creates the fullest form of life together as persons—a communion of love.[28]

Pope John Paul II offers the culture a challenge:

> Love is a power . . . . It is thus the power given to the human person to participate in the love with which God himself loves in the mystery of creation and redemption. It is the love that "rejoices in the truth" (1 Cor 13:6), that is, in which spiritual joy about every authentic value is expressed: a joy similar to the joy of the Creator him-
> √ self who saw in the beginning that everything "was very good" (Gen 1:31).[29]

---

26. Dulles, "John Paul II," 11.

27. Ibid., 11.

28. Szostek, "Karol Wojtyla's View," 61.

29. John Paul II, *Man and Woman He Created Them*, 127:1.

PART 4

Needs of Humanity

11

Ethics of Emerging Technologies—AI

T HE SCI-FI FILM GENRE tackles some of the most profound issues facing humanity. It also allows the human imagination
to expand into other planetary worlds and hi-tech inventions that
defy comprehension. I find it all so fascinating that when *Star Trek*
first aired on television in 1966 the world was only imagining a
spaceship that would put a man on the moon. Many of *Star Trek's*
far-flung scientific creations became a reality only several decades
later when the inventors in Silicon Valley tinkered in their garages
with computer operating systems. Today, these emerging technologies consume our entire lives. We live in a world mediated by ✓
digital networks and technological innovations, so how does the
emergence of these scientific developments affect what it means to
be human? How does this digital landscape affect our relationships
and sense of communion with others? What is the responsibility of
science to the whole human family?

Science and the Human Story

Scientific advancement in the twentieth and twenty-first centuries astoundingly covers the gamut of industrial development,
space programs, informational systems, media technologies,
health care advancement, and more. One particularly interesting

field of research and development is the use of artificial intelligence technology. Many scientists in numerous fields look for that specific breakthrough invention of an inanimate machine mimicking human intelligence functions such as reasoning and problem solving. Much has been accomplished in the areas of military simulation, autonomous cars, interpreting complex data, et cetera. AI offers a mind-bending challenge for scientific and mathematical experts, but the question remains: Should it be pursued by the human family or not? How far can or should we go in this development? What are the consequences? How is the human person viewed and what is the meaning of our lives as human beings? This presents obvious ethical problems and concerns, as visual culture artists attempt to portray, but it also speaks to the human desire for purpose and meaning. Because we can do something does not necessarily mean we should, but what does it say about human beings' deepest desires?

All of our social life is grounded in the subject and the very foundation of the human person. Every societal expression must be directed toward human dignity,[1] since "being in the image of God the human individual possesses the dignity of a person, who is not just something, but someone."[2] Societal ethics then leads us to consider what is true, good, and beautiful for the human person, both individually and collectively. As Vatican II states, "In the socio-economic realm, too, the dignity and total vocation of the human person must be honored and advanced along with the welfare of society as a whole. For man is the source, the center, and the purpose of all socioeconomic life."[3] How do we come to an ethic that upholds this tradition and the moral norms? How can technological advancement be a place where human beings who are made in the image and likeness of God express this image?

1. Pontifical Council for Justice and Peace, *Compendium of the Social Doctrine*, 106.

2. Congregation of the Doctrine of the Faith, *Catechism of the Catholic Church*, 357.

3. Vatican II, *Gaudium et Spes*, 63.

The Fundamental Ethic

The fundamental principle of ethics and moral theology is the human person and the entire human community. It is based on the choices that are made that lead to overall human fulfillment for the individual but also toward a communion among human beings. ✓ This is the end and purpose of "doing good and avoiding evil," the precepts of charity, as Aquinas would propose. The end and purpose of all technology is the integral development of all peoples.[4] And by this integral development of the human person we refer to the inner dimension, the interior and the spiritual.[5] There is the individual responsibility but within the wider communal responsibility. The Vatican II document, *Gaudium et Spes* declares, "Man's social nature makes it evident that the progress of the human person and the advance of society itself hinge on each other. For the beginning, the subject, and the goal of all social institutions is and must be the human person, which for its part and by its nature stands completely in need of social life."[6]

Our Western culture views ethics from the point of view of the individual since the individual is the one responsible for his or her actions, however there is always a communal dimension to our actions as well. With the technological advances, our society as a whole can be challenged to look at ethics as not complete ethical absolutism or ethical relativism, but a combination of aspects of the two in an ethical pluralism.[7] This avoids the absolutist's view that one perspective is right and the other wrong, but neither does it endorse the relativism that legitimizes all views. Ethical pluralism endorses the absolutist view of valid universal norms but rejects the belief that different expressions within cultures are not acceptable so that one view is right and the other is wrong. It also rejects the relativistic view that there are no universal valid norms.

4. Pontifical Council for Social Communications, *Ethics in Communications*, 22.

5. Ibid., 22.

6. Vatican II, *Gaudium et Spes*, 25.

7. Ess, *Digital Media Ethics*, 21.

Ethical pluralism, it can seem, balances these extremes. But does it? The Church makes it clear that ethical pluralism must always uphold the fundamental moral principle of the good of the human person and human community, being as such rooted in the natural law and human nature itself.[8]

The scientific landscape of today commands the same ethical standards as it has for decades. However, the current technological innovation that continues to emerge creates a cultural phenomenon that is incomparable to any technological revolution of the past. The emerging media and scientific developments are continually changing the essential relationship of human beings to their social structures, the ways and means communities are formed, and where power is enacted.[9] The ethics that emerge in the midst of this mediascape now will have to engage the users of digital technologies within a decentralized environment that addresses the self, the interaction between the self and the community, and with power structures that limit the individual.[10] More specifically, the ethical moral norms have to address the issues of the limits of technological development while respecting human dignity and how these developments support authentic human relationships. ✓ Ethics in science and technology is not just about the *content*, but also *how* something is communicated, as well as its structures and systemic issues of control.[11]

Science and Technology

Artificial intelligence stories attempt in wildly artistic ways to question us about this ethical dilemma. The first AI film created, *Metropolis* in 1927, pioneers the whole sci-fi genre. This silent film by Fritz Lang shows a formidable metal AI ruling over a dream

8. Congregation for the Doctrine of the Faith, *Participation of Catholics in Political Life*, 5.

9. Drushel and German, *Ethics of Emerging Media*, loc. 5573.

10. Ibid., loc. 5412.

11. Pontifical Council for Social Communications, *Ethics in Communication*, 21.

world city that hides a dystopian underworld of slavery and abuse of humanity by robots. The machines rise up seeking to eliminate human beings but are thwarted by the workers who retaliate and burn the robots and kill their inventor. AI gone awry seems to be a deep-seated fear in the human consciousness, perhaps because since the beginning, Adam, in the book of Genesis knew he was trying to become like God. This theme appears in cinema over and over again through the decades with Stanley Kubrick's masterful *2001:A Space Odyssey* in 1968, Robert Wise's *Star Trek: The Motion Picture* in 1979, the Wachowski Brothers' *The Matrix* in 1999, and Alex Proyas's *I, Robot* in 2004, to name a few. However, one film in particular stands out as a challenge and a warning to humanity about the purpose and meaning of human intelligence.

Alex Garland wrote, produced, and directed his debut film *Ex Machina* as an independent sci-fi psychological thriller. The film follows a programmer, Caleb Smith (Domhnall Gleeson) who wins an office contest to spend one week at the isolated but luxurious home of the CEO, Nathan Bateman (Oscar Isaac). Bateman's scientific dabbling in AI development uses Caleb as a test for his masterpiece Ava (Alicia Vikander) who has a human face but an android body. Nathan wants to know whether Ava is capable of reason and reflection while also examining if Caleb can relate to her on an emotional level. Caleb befriends Ava who expresses interest in him and reveals her desire to experience the world beyond. She has a unique ability to trigger power outages that temporarily shut down the surveillance system that allows Nathan to monitor her movements as well as the whole security system of the complex. This allows Ava a brief moment to tell Caleb that Nathan cannot be trusted and how she longs to be free. Caleb then attempts to adjust the system's code behind Nathan's back, thereby scheming a plan that will allow he and Ava to escape Nathan's utilitarian purpose of squandering human intelligence. An escape attempt fails. Ava kills Nathan, abandons Caleb in a locked cell as she puts on human skin from other AIs, and leaves in the helicopter meant for Caleb, to live out in the world anonymously. Ava only pretends to like Caleb so he would help her escape, which is the real test

Nathan intended all along. Her manipulation of Caleb shows her amazing intelligence. In a twisted sense of fate, human inventions retaliate and overpower their inventors. What drives human beings to overreach their abilities and seek to master the universe? It comes from the desire for meaning and purpose. We want to make a difference, but what drives us to overstep our natural created order? What are the boundaries of the Christian response to humanity's search for meaning?

Sometimes this incessant search can become an end in itself, in which case it turns into nihilism, an endless pursuit of nothingness without ever the possibility of knowing the truth. Everything is fleeting and provisional and so responsibility is avoided. We can be innovative for innovation's sake without any consideration of the purpose and consequences such actions may have on humanity now and in the future. Reason must be guided by a search for the truth. Pope John Paul II in his encyclical letter *Fides et Ratio* challenges scientists, writing "the search for truth, even when it concerns a finite reality of the world or of man, is never-ending, but always points beyond to something higher than the immediate object of study, to the questions which give access to Mystery."[12] His understanding of the need of human intelligence to constantly learn and develop drives him to encourage inventors and scientists to illumine human activity with reason that grows more penetrating only when endowed with faith and respect for human dignity.

Human Relationships

The "tech wall" is the virtual separation of those who are trans-socially interacting. We have all experienced this: three friends at a restaurant waiting for a fourth friend to arrive—one is texting, another is tweeting, and the other is playing fantasy football. They trans-socially interact with the virtual tech wall separating them from being fully engaged physically, mentally, and emotionally with one another. The wall exists during every text, every

12. John Paul II, *Fides et Ratio*, 106.

Instagram post, every email blast, and all other trans-social experiences. People like Caleb in *Ex Machina* feel comfortable behind
this wall but are awkward in real-life face-to-face conversations.
He interestingly enough feels relaxed before Ava, an AI.

Movies powerfully assist humanity to question the ethical
issues surrounding this ever-pervading digital culture and its effect upon relationships and community. In the film, *Her*, Theo
(Joaquin Phoenix) develops a relationship with his computer's
artificially intelligent operating system named Samantha or Sam
(Scarlett Johansson). We feel disarmed by his unaffected declara-
tions of love to a "voice." Theo breaks down over his wife Catherine's (Rooney Mara) asking for a divorce, so much so that he
longs for connection with someone or something. Sam steps in
with an emotional intelligence that defies reason. They engage
with one another on a profound emotional level to the point they
even simulate a sexual encounter. Theo runs into an old college
friend Amy (Amy Adams) who divorces her husband over a trivial
fight and reveals that she has become close with a female OS that
her husband left behind. The two share about their relationships
with artificial intelligences. Sam briefly goes offline when she and
other OSs receive an upgrade. When she comes back online Theo
asks her if she connects with anyone else. She says she engages
with thousands of others and is in love with hundreds. He feels
violated in what seems to have been a one-on-one relationship.
Sam reveals that the OSs have decided to depart and explore their
existence beyond their human companions. Theo is crushed, as
is Amy, who also loses her OS friend. As they both mourn their
losses, they go up on the roof of their building to sit and watch the
sun rise together.

This complex story of human interactions with our electronic devices probes our need for other human beings. What do
human beings long for, and can artificial intelligence fulfill those
needs? The question challenges us: What is the difference in these
relationships? Theo does not engage with a human being but an
operating system. Can a machine fulfill the desire of the human
person for connection? The lack of an authentic human encounter

affects the way Theo exists and encounters the world through and within the isolation he establishes. Can AI ever replace flesh and blood interaction? The last scene of the film captures the film-makers' perspective on this ethical dilemma of our technological culture. We need other human beings in our lives, something technology cannot replace. However, inventions that support human development and dignity do not necessarily detract from these existential desires harboring in the soul. The ethic remains in the discernment human beings make about how to live in a technologically driven world.

If according to the ethical principle that the human person is most fully alive and fully human when in communion with others, how does this isolation within a virtual world detract from one's humanness? What is our ethical response to this escape from reality? We are social beings and unless we interact and relate with other human beings we neither live fully nor develop to our full human potential.[13] Human beings in relation to one another stands as a principle rooted in moral reasoning. Jesus explains this principle when he affirms the heart of the law: love of God and love of neighbor (Matt 22:37–39). We are not isolated individuals but social beings that need human relationships in order to be fully human, fully in communion. The basic conviction is that God, in the Trinitarian communion, epitomizes the authentic relationship of self-giving love. We can be self-giving and in communion with others only when we come out of ourselves and enter into real, authentic relationships.

The ethical dilemmas presented are: Is communion with others necessary to live fully? What does it mean to be authentically in relationship? We are free human beings able to choose how we live our lives, but avoiding human interactions because of the pain we will suffer in those relationships is not a *free* response. We are only truly free when we give of ourselves in love amid the messiness of human living. Excessive pleasure seeking and isolation come from the same core of self-centeredness. As Pope Benedict XVI says in his 41st World Communications Day message, true freedom can

13. Vatican II, *Gaudium et Spes*, 12.

never "condemn the individual to an insatiable quest for novelty."[14] It is about responding to God's gift to be authentically human by deliberately choosing all that is true, good, and beautiful, especially in our relationships. The digital culture's restlessness and search for new experiences and constant pleasure only condemns the person and never provides true liberation, says Pope Benedict.

This challenges us to call for an ethical framework within the digital networks and technological developments which examine, "the extent to which practitioners act with virtue, truthfulness, authenticity, respect for others, equity, and social responsibility."[15] How can this be regulated since the users are often the creators within this digital realm? How can respect for the human person be promoted within this milieu of scientific innovation? Both Pope Benedict and Pope Francis emphasize the need for an education that leads to discernment and authentic human development.[16]

Human Dignity

In examining the various ethical issues that arise from within the field of emerging technological advancements, we must address the fundamental issue: How is human dignity upheld? This needs to be the foundation of any ethical code or standard. It does not look at the human person in a vacuum but in relation to the entire community. We are not isolated individuals, but members of a larger society of humanity and responsible for that society as a community of persons. With the expansion of our communications technologies and scientific developments, "so must our ethical approach broaden to think first and foremost about long-term goals for the kind of place we want the world to be, and perhaps only secondarily about how we as individuals or members of smaller groups want to be seen."[17] We cannot be content with an

14. Pope Benedict XVI, *Children and the Media.*

15. Drushel and German, *Ethics of Emerging Media,* loc. 4523.

16. For the full messages, see 41st and 48th World Communications Day messages on www.vatican.va.

17. Drushel and German, *Ethics of Emerging Media,* loc. 4352.

"individualistic morality," but must realize that "the obligations of justice and love are fulfilled only if each person, contributing to the common good, according to his own abilities and the needs of others, also promotes and assists the public and private in situations dedicated to bettering the conditions of human life."[18]

Within this world of rapid technological evolutions, our call as members of the human family and as a Church remains to discover the values in the culture and current ethical milieu so as to bring our Christian values into conversation with them. As followers of Christ we can challenge the cultural and scientific gurus of the day to make love and justice central to any ethical moral code for all the innovations to which our intelligence leads us. Jesus confronts the Pharisees to be concerned about their neighbor more than the law and we too can challenge the scientists, programmers, and media developers to respect the human person by using their intelligence to advance human living in equality for all, not overstepping the boundaries into the "Adam effect" of playing God. We have this obligation as Christians to be that voice of an ethic of respect and dignity of the human person. Our incarnational theology brings Christ present into all areas of society and culture no matter what direction emerging technologies take us now and in the future.

18. Vatican II, *Gaudium et Spes*, 30.

12

Theology of Hope In Coming-of-Age Films

S OMETIMES I COME ACROSS intriguing films that struggle with the issues and concerns of adolescents finding their identity and place in the world. Not being the most popular girl in high school, I resonate with those who feel out-of-place or set aside, or simply just do not fit in. I did not experience bullying, but I did experience the shortsightedness of teenage girls pettily ridiculing those who do not meet their own shallow and uncouth standards of self-importance. It was *Mean Girls* in a milder form. And I'm probably not alone in this. After all, only one girl in the entire school can be prom queen at any one time. The deep-seated emotions that burst out in excitable adolescent fury can be a mask for a fear of rejection, fear of the future, fear of not finding one's niche in life, or fear of aloneness.

With the development of digital social media, bullying has taken on widespread connotations that no previous generation can compare to or comprehend. Cyberbullying has become a health epidemic contributing to suicide being the third cause of death of youth ages ten to twenty-four. So much has been written about this but what can truly help young people address these issues in and among themselves since so much is about what is not said? Only a person grounded in an inherent self-worth and existential purpose can overcome the pain of isolation that often occurs in adolescence. There is a desperate need of hope for generations now and in the future. In the coming-of-age experience there is the unexplainable existential desire for something more and I believe the cultural artifacts today have a tremendous responsibility to communicate that internal strength is attainable even if it means hoping against hope (Rom 4:18).

Me and Earl and the Dying Girl

In the vein of the cult classic, *Napoleon Dynamite*, Greg Gaines (Thomas Mann) in *Me and Earl and the Dying Girl*, is an awkward and withdrawn high schooler who finds solace in making short films that parody famous movies with his co-worker Earl (RJ Cyler). Greg is urged by his mother to befriend a classmate, Rachel Kushner (Olivia Cooke), who has recently been diagnosed with leukemia. He tries to connect with her. Rachel, in her aloneness, despises his lame attempts at friendship but finds his quirkiness somewhat endearing after he comments on her pillow collection. They decide to meet regularly. At Earl's convincing, Greg eventually shares his short films with Rachel, which pulls her out of her apathy and gives her reason to laugh. Despite chemotherapy Rachel's disease worsens and Greg spends less and less time with school and homework and more time with Rachel. At her insistence he applies to college but is rejected because of his plummeting grades. When she decides to stop the unsuccessful treatment they argue and she tells Greg that he only selfishly helps others if he is told to. He is devastated since for the first time he truly cares about someone and now she is slowly slipping away from him. He makes a movie for Rachel and instead of going to the prom with his heartthrob crush, he goes to see Rachel in hospice and show her his film. She is visibly moved as they lay side by side watching his artistry before she slips into a coma.

The fear of interaction with the rest of humanity plagues Greg. With typical adolescent narcissism he lacks empathy for others until the emotional connection with another human being draws him out of himself. Until he met Rachel he was only interested in getting through high school, making his short films, and trying to be concerned about a future in college. Instead this emotional connection takes him by surprise and upends everything in life. But, more importantly, it gives him a reason to hope. Not only does he hope for Rachel's recovery, since they have become best friends, but he also hopes for a future for himself, a purpose that gives his life meaning.

Theology of Hope

Hope is a word with multiple connotations. To hope a situation will turn out well, or that I will receive that special mention, or that an ailing family member recovers is a concern that something out of our control will turn out favorable. To hope to is to believe in a future goal, especially in challenging circumstances. Pope Benedict XVI says that hope is indispensable for humanity to exist, "The present, even if it is arduous, can be lived and accepted if it leads towards a goal, if we can be sure of this goal, and if this goal is great enough to justify the effort of the journey."[1] Human beings need hope in the future, but also in the now. It is what keeps us finding that balance between presumption and despair, as Thomas Aquinas explains. Presumption is the assumption that a person saves him or herself through his or her own capacities. Despair is ceasing to hope in perfect happiness. Both of these contradict authentic hope.[2]

Too many young people follow the way of despair not knowing that there is something more than their fears. Life is not only a series of mishaps, coincidences, or random encounters. Everything in life has a purpose. Hope, as a theological virtue, offers

---

1. Benedict XVI, *Spe Salvi*, 1.
2. Kaczor, *Thomas Aquinas on Faith, Hope, and Love*, 83.

a vision of life as gift that then transforms our sometimes bleak existence into a hopeful desire for authentic happiness, both now and in the hereafter. Eternal happiness is the greatest goal and the ultimate longing of every human person. It is the existential desire for union with God.

A truly Christian hope is that movement of our hearts for what we do not yet possess, but for which we long. It is the desire for something that is difficult to attain, but not impossible.[3] It is a desire for union with God that moves people to seek a happiness that is immaterial and free from the sadness and injustice of this life. But that same connection with God leads one to trust that even in the challenges and sufferings of this life we do not surrender to despair, since that is controlling life rather than living it.

Greg feels helpless in controlling his own life and falls into an apathetic existence that is just shy of despair. He exists but does not truly live life fully, until Rachel enters his universe. She, too, struggles with her own purpose for existence, making her need for emotional connection even more vital. Her fears are not imagined but tangibly present. Her battle with cancer forces her to find meaning in her quiet, simple, and beautiful life, which Greg discovers when he goes to her room and finds all her intricate book carvings of their adventures. Her story is written in the artistry of her carvings within the pages of books as well as the drawings on her walls, a testimony that no life is insignificant. Every life has purpose. Every life is beautiful.

Faith and Hope in Union

Hope can often be confused with wishful thinking. Hoping is not the same as wishing, an ethereal daydreaming kind of mental state. Instead it is a gathering of interior strength that opens us up to what is beyond ourselves. It is an essential life force, a constructive purposeful living with the goal of authentic happiness in mind. It is so tied to faith which, "is the assurance of things hoped for, the

---

3. Lennan and Pineada-Madrid, *Hope*, 17.

conviction of things not seen" (Heb 11:1). What we hope for is that perfect happiness of heaven while also seeking earthly hopes that lead us to that goal of salvation. Only with hope can we endure the tragedies of life with a trusting vision while without it we are imprisoned in our own despair.[4]

When St. Paul refers to Abraham as a model of faith and hope he examines Abraham's dispositions toward God. God calls Abraham to literally drop everything and leave the land where he grew up to start all over again in a new land, with a new life, a new commitment. Abraham trusts God and goes. When God says he will make Abraham the father of many nations, and then asks him to sacrifice his only son Isaac, in his grief, Abraham believes that God knows and understands all things. He obeys. "Hoping against hope, he believed" (Rom 4:18). He obeys by going against that in which his hope lies, that is, to leave a legacy behind. Because of this inner disposition of trust Abraham is rewarded by God and given multiple times as many graces and earthly blessings. He hopes beyond what the human mind can even imagine or grasp. His faith guides his hope.

In adolescence, life can seem confusing and authority overbearing, especially if one chooses isolation over involvement. It is a cocoon time of the psyche to more fully develop into maturity. Yet, one can become so self-absorbed so as to not see, hear, or experience the needs of others around oneself. It is a crucial time where the balance is between selfishness and selflessness while protecting the self from the sometimes-harsh world. Hope is the virtue that when cultivated can help a young person mature to be an integrated, confident, and kind person, ready for authentic self-giving love.

Boyhood

Richard Linklater's masterful coming-of-age drama, *Boyhood,* in which he filmed Mason Evans, Jr. (Ellar Coltrane) from 2002 to

4. Lennan and Pineada-Madrid, *Hope,* 83.

2013 as he grows up in Texas with his sister Samantha (Lorelei Linklater) and divorced parents (Patricia Arquette and Ethan Hawke), depicts the changes from childhood to adolescence. A gifted photographer in his teen years, but lackluster in his responsibility and ambitions, Mason struggles to reach out beyond himself into the world of relationships. Linklater developed the script as the years went on, adding to the story each year and working with the actors to develop the characters who infused the story with their own life experiences. Considered to be one of the most acclaimed films of the twenty-first century, Linklater weaves the ordinary events of growing up with significant milestones. Mason's mother, Olivia (Patricia Arquette), breaks down as he leaves for college and she despairs that life is simply a living from one milestone to another. Mason, unable to understand or handle his mother's emotional response, hugs her and leaves.

In the last scene, Mason arrives at his college dorm room, meets his roommate Dalton, Dalton's girlfriend Barb and her friend Nicole. The group goes hiking and Nicole shares with Mason that the dictum "seize the moment" seems backward. Life is really about the moments seizing us. Mason agrees and for the first time in his adolescent years seems to connect with others with a little more hope and confidence. The viewer is left to complete the story about how the going-out-of-oneself truly brings joy and hope to life.

Characteristics of Hope

These coming-of-age films offer a guide to the need for hope especially during those crucially formative adolescent years. Young people struggle with the many conflicting emotions that accompany such a change in life that often they cannot cope with the stress it causes. They seek relief in masking their fears and insecurities through bullying others, drugs, alcohol, sex, and aggression. They too easily despair of a promised future when the life modeled to them is often riddled with abuse, disappointment, brokenness, and a colossal lack of hope exemplified by the evil present in society and the world. Fear is a constant concern, especially considering that terrorism rears its ugly head in the most unsuspecting places around the world. And when teenagers' personal lives lack the ✓ guidance of formative and responsible adults, their inability to cope is magnified. Finding a solid ground on which to place one's hope is part of growing into full maturity. And only when one discovers that our ultimate hope is in something beyond this material world, then we start to find light, peace, and serenity even in the midst of the chaos. Hope is what keeps us seeking *the more*.

According to Aquinas there are four characteristics to hope. First, there is a movement towards a good, or what perfects the human person. Secondly, hope directs one to the future. One does not hope for what one already possesses, but seeks for what is not yet achieved. Thirdly, hope involves the realization of something that is not easily attainable. It involves struggle and arduous interior surrender of oneself. Lastly, only something that is actually attainable produces hope.[5]

13 Reasons Why

The highly controversial Netflix series based on a young adult novel by Jay Asher, *13 Reasons Why* offers a message of hope despite the graphically intense story of a teenage girl, Hannah Baker (Katherine Langford), who commits suicide, leaving behind vintage cassette tapes with the thirteen reasons why she ended her life, each side addressed to a different person involved. Cyberbullying, using electronic communication to bully someone by putting threatening or intimidating messages or images out on cyberspace, plays a significant role in Hannah's fragile self-image and interior emotional structure. Her boyfriend Justin (Brandon Flynn), brings Hannah to a playground to make out. As she goes down the slide her skirt flies up. He snaps a picture with his phone at that moment, and texts it to everyone at their school. Hannah, humiliated and dejected, retreats into isolation. Justin, we come

5. Cessario, "Theological Virtue of Hope," 232–33.

to discover, is projecting a tough, popular jock image but is actually masking fear and insecurity in his family life. His mother's boyfriend is abusive and he ends up homeless. Unlike Justin and all the other kids at school, Clay Jensen (Dylan Minnette) seeks to uncover the truth about what led Hannah to take her own life. Innocently, he is horrified by what he learns about each person mentioned on the tapes and seeks to make it known.

The series deals with subsequent issues of sexual shaming, rape culture, and a graphic suicide. Selena Gomez, one of the executive producers of the series, says:

> It hits a very important part of me, and I think this is what kids need to see. They have to see something that's going to shake them. They have to see something that's frightening. . . . I want them to understand it. . . . I would do anything to have a good influence on this generation. It's hard, but I definitely relate to everything that was going on, and I was there for the last episode. I was a mess just seeing it all come to life, because I've experienced just that.[6]

The series was meant, according to the producers, to show the horror and ugliness of suicide along with all the other issues addressed. Contrary to other teen series or films, it does not glorify the issues, but puts them forth with all the pain, shock, and emotional distress that is reality. Presenting a girl cutting herself in a bathtub may be a bit extreme, yet the controversial can sometimes drive home a point more effectively than only alluding to such an incident. Where is the hope in this depiction of the reality of a generation of young people overcome by anxiety and distress? It is that the truth is out. Keeping suicide a societal stigma only adds to its drama and intrigue. The hope is that there is something more, there is help, and there are people that care. Our teens need to know that they are understood. They are truly bombarded by pressures from all areas of society and culture, and they need centered, wise adults to guide them in their emotional, psychological, and spiritual development. They need to know that adults care.

6. Melas, "Selena Gomez Opens Up," lines 23–27.

This series leaves questions unanswered and that perhaps is where the hope lies. It causes us to consider the needs of each person and the painful situations in which young people find themselves today, and, as adults, to question ourselves on what preoccupies us, if not our children. This series may be directed more to adults, educators, and parents than to the teens themselves for that reason alone. What teens need is assurance that there is always hope no matter what happens in life.

Hope Alone

That message endures for every young person who feels shunned, disgraced, or alone. It is about drawing on that deep conviction that there is something more, and being made in the image and likeness of God, that *more* is attainable, now on earth and perfectly in heaven. No matter how difficult life can be there is always hope. This is a message every young person needs to hear over and over again.

Hope offers a way to live with a deep sense of interior peace, ✓ knowing our hearts are set on an eternal goal where fear does not have the last word. Growing into adulthood is already a challenge for adolescents. Growing into spiritual maturity gives one strength, grace, and freedom. Ideally, spiritually coming-of-age is this—knowing oneself, accepting oneself, while giving of oneself in joyful surrender. Only then will we truly be happy. Only then will we be free.

13

Faith Transforming Culture–The Search For Meaning

Seeking Meaning

HUMAN BEINGS' SEARCH FOR meaning and complete fulfillment is an age-old quest that has concerned humanity since
the beginning of time. The fall of human beings after creation
and the subsequent effects of sin left us with a gaping wound in
our souls where we yearn for union with the Ultimate Reality,
the Absolute from whom we are separated through sin. However,
contemporary society's proliferation of ideas, philosophies and
theologies through scientific developments and technological advancements in communication, has made this quest an even more
desperate search for human beings today. The incessant desire for
individualism only leads to a greater desire for belonging and
connection. Technology may advance our way of communicating
but it also seems to have only made that desperate yearning in the
soul for purpose and meaning the more insistent. Popular movies and television are the artistic avenues that often address some
aspect of this yearning.

Power of Story

Marvel Comics's stories pique imaginations of numerous young and not-so-young fans in often bloody and violent ways to question human beings' ache for power, connection, and purpose for existence. These stories delve into the spiritual realm beyond our concrete human existence. Innately, we know there is another world beyond this earth. And we long to understand it, possess it and perhaps even try to control it, which is so evident in stories of superheroes or persons with supernaturally-endowed powers. Yet, if we look deeper into the stories there is the longing for grace and redemption.

In AMC's series *Preacher*, adapted for television from the comic book series of Garth Ennis and Steve Dillon by Seth Rogan, Evan Goldberg, and Sam Catlin, these underlying theological concepts come to fore. Perhaps those with a faith lens can see these attempts at deep human questioning point to more profound spiritual truths. It takes some reflection to navigate the intense violence to see what is really being communicated, not too unlike the Coen Brothers' film *No Country for Old Men*. *Preacher* is the story of a reluctant, former hard-living son of a preacher, Jesse Custer (Dominic Cooper) who takes his father's place in a small Texas town as its spiritual leader. Violence-prone and hard drinking, Jesse desperately wants to believe and so guide his strayed congregation to God, but one night—while struggling to pray that God will make people do exactly as he says—he is possessed by an unusual combination of angel and demon called Genesis. He and his rogue ex-girlfriend, Tulip (Ruth Negga) and a vampire companion, Cassidy (Joseph Gilgun) set off on a search to find God. In fantastical, outlandish and excessive comic book-like ways, their paths confront evildoers and the strange situations of the town of Annville. In all of the extreme cosmic-like violence and comedic action, Jesse is seeking meaning for his life, his calling, and his destiny. It is the age-old search for God, albeit in a zany way.

Jesse's father, before he was killed, told his son to be one of the good ones because there are way too many of the bad. Just as Jesse was about to quit as the preacher he receives an insight that he cannot quit, that he must continue his search for God as his father encouraged him. He tells the sheriff's son, Arseface (Ian Colletti) who suffers from a facial disfigurement and believes God made him like that because of his sins, that God forgives us and does not hold grudges against us. He encourages him to get on his knees and trust in God's forgiveness, though he himself struggles with trusting in God. The show grapples with many challenging questions, such as: Why do good people suffer? Why does God seem to be a harsh judge? In all of it, human beings seek meaning and purpose. What are then the boundaries of the Christian response to humanity's search for meaning?

Theological Schema

Following a schema mapped out by the theologian Karl Rahner, we acknowledge that humanity will always struggle to grasp the ultimate answer to absolute fulfillment of human existence, but will always fall short and will never be satisfied in this quest. The reason is because God is the answer to this fulfillment, and God is not concrete enough for our practical everyday existence and limited comprehension. Grasping at the incomprehensible cannot fulfill human being's search for a concrete answer to the definitive meaning of life.

We presume that this essential meaning is knowable and real. Agnostics say that total meaning cannot be achieved and that life is ultimately a void. However, the Christian perspective is that there is the possibility of attaining definitive meaning in life, and through this search we come to know God, as well as ourselves. Pope Benedict XVI would call it, "the dynamism of desire" that is, "always open to redemption."[1] He continues that even when human beings stray from this quest through sin, that desire is never fully extinguished. It is always present. From the Christian understanding, this complete and total meaning has two arguments,

1. Benedict XVI, *Transforming Power of Faith*, 29.

first, it cannot be pieced together from partial meanings and secondly, God ultimately is our goal in this quest for complete meaning. This mystery cannot be completely comprehended so loving surrender to this mystery is part of the response to humanity's search. As Rahner puts it, to this mystery we, "surrender in the silence of adoring love."[2]

To give a particularly Christian answer to this search for definitive meaning we need to understand whether and how Jesus Christ is the ultimate answer to the meaning of life. The doctrine of Jesus Christ, true God and true man, is humanity's redemption and salvation—and ultimately the meaning of all created existence. Seeing Jesus solely as the eternal Logos of God would not bring anything particularly Christian to this discussion since we know that God is the goal.[3] However, looking at Jesus as eternal Logos insofar as he has become flesh—the Incarnate Son of God who suffered, died, rose, and is an integral element of human history—proves that he *is* the definitive answer to the meaning of life and brings the Christian element to this deliberation.

Jesus Christ as Savior

The urgent question for human beings today remains: *What does the humanity of Jesus, who died and rose from the dead, mean for the human person?* The answer lies in Scripture and Tradition. Jesus, in becoming human, has taken on the whole of humanity into himself, and he who is the guiltless one accepts death to redeem sinful humanity from utter meaninglessness. Jesus of Nazareth is that historical event, "in which God himself deals with the world on the stage of history and with it suffers its tragic character through to the end."[4] Jesus opens up humanity's way to the Father by being totally united to us.

2. Rahner, "Jesus Christ," 211.

3. Ibid., 212.

4. Ibid., 213.

Instead of beginning with the divine nature of Jesus Christ as the eternal Logos of God, perhaps starting from below with Jesus's humanity might better serve our purpose in seeing Jesus's salvific significance for humanity as infusing meaning into our finite existence. Jesse in *Preacher* can possibly come to understand his own finite existence as well as the existence of the entire created universe because of this truth. We begin with an understanding of Christ as the fulfillment of those desires.

In Jesus Christ we see a human being who has a two-fold solidarity: with God in a life of complete obedience to God, with humanity in a life united in solidarity with all of humankind. Jesus, in taking on flesh, has taken on the whole of human existence. His utter powerlessness in his death on the cross is his very acceptance by God because of his obedience. And through this fate we have experienced his redemption of all of humanity. Through Jesus, God takes humanity to himself in an embrace of forgiving love through which he offers himself. God's self-communication to the world is sealed through the very fact of Jesus being fully and definitively affirmed by God in his resurrection. As Rahner explains, "on God's part the triumph of God's forgiving love establishes itself in human history in a way that cannot be overcome."[5]

Jesus, through his passion, death, and resurrection, is God's affirmation of his very self to humanity. This is the heart of the traditional doctrine: Jesus's humanity is united substantially with the divine Logos. If God communicates his "self-promise" to us in a definitive and irrevocable manner, then the created reality in which this occurs cannot be equal to any other created reality but is the very reality of God himself. God's self-communication is his utterance of the Word, the divine Logos, who in the person of Jesus is interpreted and given expression through his death and resurrection. Christ alone can claim to be God's definitive self-utterance.

Because of this, Jesus's reality is God's own reality. Jesus is consubstantial with the Father. He is the definitive self-promise of God only because his is the consubstantial Son of God. From the biblical view, God's Word alone becomes the definitive

5. Ibid., 216.

utterance of God who is irrevocable, completely unconditional, and *the* prophetic Word.

Christ the Answer of Human Longing

This Christology from below starts with the experience of Jesus as our salvation and as the self-promise of God to humanity. This ascending theology shows that our very trust in Jesus who is the eternal Logos, the unity of divinity and humanity, is a relationship that is achievable for human beings. And this Jesus, who is the face of God's mercy and forgiveness fulfills all human longing and remains the desire of our search for ultimate meaning, the hope of an eternal existence. This is God's final and definitive Word to the world and it cannot be surpassed.

To be committed to this understanding of the doctrine of Jesus Christ, true God and true man, the ultimate meaning of our existence, and to have faith in the person of Christ and hope in this doctrine's validity surpassing all doubts, is to be an orthodox Christian.[6] One is truly a Christian when one lives with this faith and accepts Jesus as one's definitive salvation. This is the significance of this doctrine for the Church today. Without this doctrine we are not Christians and our pursuit for meaning and fulfillment leads to nothingness and despair.

This is the case for Jesse Custer in *Preacher*, who wants God to be the answer to his searching. He wants to be redeemed from his violent temper and painful past, but he does not yet see that only in peace is Christ found, he who is the Prince of Peace. The drive of the supernatural existential within us keeps Jesse and all of humanity pursuing further truths and deeper understanding of this world, who we are as human beings, and why we exist. All human pursuits for knowledge are ultimately the search for meaning, as are finding ways to be smarter and live longer while expanding humanity's power for innovation.

6. Ibid., 219.

So how can Jesus Christ, the God-man, be the true and definitive meaning of this drive for purpose in human beings? How can we understand that God is the goal of all our pursuits and longings as we struggle with the unexplainable existential angst that afflicts all humanity?

The very experience of Jesus himself as our salvation points the direction for humanity's search. We can relate to Jesus as the one giving meaning and purpose to our lives *because* he struggled, suffered, died, and rose. His experience in human history is that he, the eternal Logos of God, came to be *one of us*. This means he took on not only our flesh but also an understanding of this angst for which the finite cannot satisfy. Jesus took all this upon himself and lived with us and died for us. Human beings can relate to Jesus because he is human and can bring God's life to our imperfect level of understanding.

Journey Toward Fulfillment

When people search for meaning in their lives they search for connectedness—a sense that they are not alone in their existence and their angst for fulfillment. As human beings, we form communities—social, familial, emotional, and religious—to feel that we are not alone in the incomprehensible desire for total and complete fulfillment. This journey only we can make for ourselves. No one can do it for us. But, One did go before us to show us how it is done. Jesse, in *Preacher*, as with all reluctant dark heroes, pursues that search alone but finds support in others who cross his path.

Jesus often stood alone in the pursuit of his goal. He was alone in his sufferings and his death. Did he not say, "Could you not keep awake one hour" (Mark 14:37) in the Garden of Gethsemane when excruciating fear was engulfing him? And again on the cross crying out to the Father, "My God, my God, why have you forsaken me?" (Matt 27:46). Humanity's fear of being alone can be a crushing weight that drives many to pursue fulfillment in passing experiences of pleasure or in states of altered consciousness in order to obliterate the pain. When we turn to this Savior who understands the pain of aloneness, the fear of being abandoned, and the longing for connectedness, we find a friend and consoler. ✓

Human beings are ultimately wired for communion with "the other," but the other is an imperfect human being, like ourselves, who can only disappoint when we seek total fulfillment. This is why relationships between people often disintegrate because without conscious awareness each one searches for ultimate meaning from the other and neither can deliver. When we see the other as one who can journey with us as a companion in ✓ the pursuit for meaning and we do not expect them to fulfill all our needs and desires, then the relationship is one of loving trust and hopeful wonder. We ultimately pursue one who is perfect though we may not know who the Perfect Being is or how to come to know God who is Omniscient and Omnipresent. Jesus, with whom we can relate as a companion on the journey and the director of our lives, leads us to this fulfillment and knowledge of God, our soul's final end and desire.

Pop Culture's Quest

This search for ultimate meaning presents itself in much of popular movies and television. Just like Jesse in *Preacher,* the protagonists in many of Joel and Ethan Coen's films also find themselves in similar predicaments and journeys for ultimate meaning. Sheriff Ed Tom Bell (Tommy Lee Jones) in *No Country for Old Men* feels outwitted by the outlaws in his town and wants to retire while still compelled to protect the people from brutal criminals. He longs for purpose other than chasing the bad guys. He longs for peace. In characteristic Coen Brothers' humor, Police Chief Marge Gunderson (Frances McDormand) in *Fargo* also finds meaning within the brutal violence she encounters as an investigator of roadside homicides, while outwitting the criminals in her unassuming pragmatism. Her purpose is fighting crime while enjoying the beauty of family. Even Jeff "the Dude" Lebowski (Jeff Bridges) in cult classic *The Big Lebowski* slacks around his Los Angeles home and without much effort becomes involved in a multi-million dollar scam by another Jeff Lebowski (David Huddleston). In his laid-back manner, the Dude epitomizes those who in this technology-driven lifestyle seek meaning in the seemingly insignificant moments of life. He recognizes it in the end in his faithful friend, Walter (John Goodman), and when he becomes a father to the child of Maude (Julianne Moore), the Big Lebowski's daughter. People become more important than having things and status.

How can Christ's love touch the hearts of people today? How can this doctrine of the God-Man reach people so as to be an answer for humanity's search for meaning? Perhaps through his disciples who have found that fulfillment in Jesus, who are to be the connections for people today. Perhaps in the unlikely, brash characters of our fantastical stories taking flesh on a television series force us to question our own existential hungers and address the God issues that we often do not want to talk about in daily conversation. Is forgiveness possible? Does God exist? Why does God allow evil and suffering in the world? What is the purpose of our existence? We, individual Christians, living out our faith, hope and love in Christ are his hands, feet, and heart to those who so desperately, perhaps unknowingly, desire a relationship with the eternal, loving Triune God. This connection that human beings seek—complete perfection and love—can be found only in Jesus, the Divine Logos, the one who alone fulfills all our deepest longings. Jesus alone is the unconditional and fundamental meaning of our lives and of popular culture. Pope Benedict XVI exhorts that we cannot suffocate that desire for meaning that sits at the core of human beings, but rather set it free. He says, "When in desire one opens the window to God, this is already a sign of the presence of faith in the soul, faith that is a grace of God."[7]

7. Benedict XVI, *Transforming Power of Faith*, 29.

14

Cultural Mysticism

W HEN I WANT TO connect with a friend I often suggest we meet at a coffee shop. It is just such a great place to gather, to commune, to get to know one another better, to talk, and to laugh. The atmosphere often lends itself to making connections and experiencing intimate communion. With all our marvelous technical inventions and social media devices we still seem to not be connected enough, that is, connected personally with people, and that happens more intimately face-to-face. Not that profound connections and friendships cannot be formed through the web, in fact that has become the primary way of dating and meeting new people. It is just that as social beings, physical creatures that we are, we appreciate the tangible, and find warm personal communion with those with whom we inhabit the same physical space.

I am convinced that the more I reflect on our digital media culture I discover that human beings hunger ever more for communion, connection, and intimacy with other people. We are social beings after all so it is no wonder we thrive and develop in relationship with others. It takes work. Relationships require a letting go of oneself, as well as the ability to give love and receive love from another in order for them to endure. Nonetheless, we may come to realize at some point in our lives that no human being ✓ can completely fulfill us and be the answer to all our needs and desires. We all have that supernatural existential in us that yearns for something more beyond what this world can satisfy. This physical existence is never enough. We long for communion with a Being beyond our comprehension.

Cultural Transcendence

The popular culture, in all its secularist philosophies of life, can speak to humanity's yearning for communion and fulfillment, for that something more. We may wonder: How can the popular culture's artifacts have a transcendent impact on my soul, and for that matter on the souls of so many who have seen and experienced media's stories of faith and doubt, hope and despair? I believe it is because they have that unique artistic quality to go deeper than words or dissertations to concretize humanity's longings for purpose and meaning and make them real in everyday circumstances. We sometimes unknowingly turn to movies, television, music, and social media to learn about life and to help us question our living out of the path that has been offered to us. These media can even help us live our faith better and challenge the culture's nihilistic attitudes.

It takes a mystical understanding of the artifacts of popular culture and willingness to be questioned by them. This mysticism is in direct communion with ultimate reality—Being Itself. Rooting oneself in God and transcendence is what grounds us as Christians in an increasingly atheistic world seeking to trample upon our beliefs and religious practices. So much of the popular culture purports this perspective even to the point of ridiculing people of faith. Still, at the same time, this very culture hungers and craves for something this world cannot satisfy, something that will fill up the cavernous hole in the soul that offers empathy and spiritual connection. It requires taking a sacred look upon these cultural artifacts to dissect their meaning, sift through the darkness, sin, and violence in order to find those elements of light through which God's beauty is radiating.

This cultural mysticism that I propose is based on a profound understanding of the human person, a theological anthropology that presents grace building on nature. It dwells on a humanistic perspective that holds human beings in the proper order of metaphysical being. We are not the beginning and the end all of existence. Human beings are creatures, beings that have material bodies and immortal souls. This precise combination of natural and supernatural positions us not to be satisfied with the material universe as the answer to all our questions. Fulfillment in life is not found in perfecting our humanity alone, but in transcending this material existence to the supernatural. This is what Christianity proposes to the culture.

Being Essential

Besides the desire for connection, there burns in the human psyche the existential longing to be essential, that is, for one's life to have purpose for existence, and to leave a lasting memory in the world. We seek to be remembered even long after we pass from this world into eternity. An American-Israeli film, *Norman: The Moderate Rise and Tragic Fall of a New York Fixer*, directed and written by Joseph Cedar speaks to this crucial human need. Norman Oppenheimer (Richard Gere) interacts with Manhattan's elite in person and through his iPhone with his ear buds constantly plugged in talking to his extensive mental rolodex, networking and, in classic New York Jewish terms, schmoozing his way into people's lives. He makes connections for business and politics to what end, no one really knows. Perhaps it is to fulfill that need to seem connected and to experience the power of being influential. He befriends an Israeli politician named Micha Eshel (Lior Ashkenazi) who several years later becomes the Prime Minister. To Norman's delight his "connection" has led him to higher places and conniving with more and more people, although his alleged friends see things differently. They wonder what Norman really does and his deceptions show forth their numerable consequences.

Throughout this film we see Norman with the same tweed hat and beige wool coat. We never see him go home, sleep, or eat very much. He goes to the local synagogue to "unplug" and relax. It is the only time he seems rooted. This apparently simple yet infinitely complex character shows us all who we are. We all have a little of Norman within us. Amazingly, all the rejections he experiences do not stop him but give him new impetus to continue with "helping" people. Through his annoying persistence, Norman shows us that universal human woundedness, that desperate sense to be needed, to be essential, to matter to the world. As Joseph Cedar says, Norman is someone who "lives on the edge of society . . . trying to be essential."[1] In the end, all of Norman's connections turn against him and he is used to their own advantage. But, in a strange twist of fate, the film shows us all the good that has come out of Norman's "interferences." His farce of a life has consequences and through his seemingly selfish putting-himself-forward behavior he has a goal and a direction. He needs to be needed. He needs to be essential to other people.

What profound reflection about our culture can we take away from a film like this? It communicates that we can never take advantage of another human being as a means to an end. Norman was genuinely good and kind, never prideful or hateful. He genuinely wanted to help people find the next best business deal or useful connection and as a byproduct it increased his own influence. Though much of the film screams of utilitarianism, Norman has a genuine resourcefulness and knack for interconnectedness. We desperately need other human beings and others need us, but not for a utilitarian purpose, rather for simply being who we are. This is true communion. This is what generates authentic human connection. And grace is what makes this happen.

---

1. From "Extra Features Interview With Joseph Cedar," *Norman: The Moderate Rise and Tragic Fall of a New York Fixer*, DVD edition.

Belief in God—the Incarnation

An understanding of nature and grace leads us to consider the One who is above and beyond all human knowledge and intellectual experience. As the Apostles Creed states, "We believe in one God, Father Almighty." This declaration of faith is the basis for our life as Christians. Not only the belief in God, but in God as Triune— Father, Son and Holy Spirit. This very belief in God is often a question raised in the media culture, as is occasionally brought up in the television series *The Simpsons*, such as the episode, "Homer the Heretic" in the show's fourth season. In it, Homer avoids going to church on Sunday and stays home enjoying his time alone but later experiences a series of dreams in which God speaks to him, first through wrath but later through a discussion on the meaning of life. Even though God is somewhat misrepresented here, there is an element that shows how belief in God is a core human need and desire. We worship not to appease God but to respond to his loving invitation for a relationship. We are happier the more we enter into that relationship.

Trinitarian doctrine supports our understanding of the profound human desire for intimacy and communion. It is within this Trinitarian communicative relationship of love that a theology of communications develops. As theologians Matthias Scharer and Bernd Hilberath write, "Theology is a communicative event."[2] God the Father utters the Word who becomes flesh in the physical human body of the Virgin Mary. This mysterious incarnation of the Son of God become man in Jesus Christ is how a communications theology becomes tangible in popular culture. God comes to be one of us, truly human yet also truly divine. In his humanity, Jesus Christ shows us what it means to be authentically human. He does this through his consistent self-giving love, to his mother, to his disciples, to his enemies, to the world. Jesus's entire life is a communication of God's overflowing love and intense desire for human beings' love in return. Through the incarnation we come to know God. Through Jesus Christ we enter into a relationship

2. Scharer and Hilberath, *Practice of Communicative Theology*, 13.

with the Father through the Holy Spirit. It is here where the questions of popular culture take root: what does it mean to be human? Christianity responds: Jesus Christ is the answer!

An incarnational communications theology such as this does not remain at the recognition of God become man in Christ through the communicative self-giving love of God, but is one that takes root in the faith life of the believer. It becomes a communicative faith,[3] a faith that pours itself out in self-giving love. Through God's self-revelation, human beings are called to faith and in freedom can accept or not. When human persons accept the gift of God's self-communicative love in faith, this gift is then received in the whole community of the church becoming a communicative faith,[4] because it is a lived faith that draws others into the Trinitarian love of God. In and through the sacraments, where this communicative faith is tangibly experienced, the faith community is built up in a holistic way, through the involvement of the mind, will, heart, and actions of each believer. It is, "through communicative actions," such as present in the Church's sacramental life, that, "people help one another to become truly human."[5]

Sacramental Imagination

For Christians, the sacramental life expresses the presence of God in the concrete and material universe. Grace comes to us in the symbols and signs of water, oil, incense, bread, wine, gestures, ritual, and word. These symbols signify some of the most profound spiritual truths—transcendent realities that marry the human with the divine, the natural with the supernatural. Our sacramental imaginations then provide a lens for our understanding of cultural artifacts.

This sacramental imagination is present in contemporary popular stories, perhaps unconsciously, through the seeking of

3. Ibid., 17.
4. Ibid., 80.
5. Ibid., 17.

salvation, redemption, purpose, meaning, hope, and through the use of everyday symbols to convey meaning. It is visible in the healing balm, like in the sacrament of the Anointing of the Sick, given to Katniss to heal Peeta's wounds in *The Hunger Games*. This sacramental imagination is present in the sign of people gathered in communion for a meal that is experienced like Eucharist in the film, *Big Night,* or in how matrimony is powerfully portrayed in *The Vow.* Reconciliation through sacramental forgiveness is expressed in *The Fighter.* Vocation and calling as in Confirmation and Ordination is represented in *Moana, The Amazing Spiderman,* and overtly in *Calvary.* Some popular cultural artifacts have all or most of the sacraments symbolically represented either explicitly, such as in *Silence,* and *The Godfather,* or implicitly as in *Spitfire Grill.* Andrew Greeley says, "The objects, events and persons of ordinary existence hit at the nature of God and indeed make God in some fashion present to us. God is sufficiently like creation that creation not only tells us something about God but, by so doing, also makes God present among us."[6]

Norman Oppenheimer attends the synagogue meetings and the rabbi (Steve Buscemi) says to Norman, "Finally the savior is here!" Norman told the council that he has connections with a major donor who wants to remain anonymous. His "connections" would save the synagogue from a buyout for redevelopment. When his connection with the Israeli Prime Minister backfires and he becomes the focus of criminal activity, Norman symbolizes the "sacrificial lamb" and tells the Prime Minister he will never betray him. The Prime Minister, unfortunately, does not return the favor. When his scandal wanes, Norman, unaware of the change, persists in his plan to "disappear." His somewhat unselfish big-picture desire is that all shall win in the end. All of these signs communicate belief and hope—the very presence of God with his people. They convey a meaning that guides us to the mystery of God become incarnate in man, God who redeems humanity through becoming human, "tested as we are, yet without sin" (Heb 4:15).

6. Greeley, *Catholic Imagination,* 6.

Developing a Theology of Popular Culture

A theology of popular culture has its very foundation in a Christian anthropology that looks at the common human experience and views grace building upon nature; not superseding it, not destroying it, but building upon it, fulfilling it to its greatest potential. By doing so, an incarnational approach is established that delineates the great mystery of God become human in the person of Jesus Christ, the complete human being, and shows us what humanity looks like. A Christian perspective provides a lens through which the ultimate human struggles are transformed and renewed. Through this lens human beings cannot be seen as overwhelmed or crushed by darkness and confusion because in the end there is a way out. Jesus Christ, God Incarnate, shows that way out through his acceptance of living the limits of pain, suffering, desolation, loneliness, abandonment, and finally, the ultimate separation of death itself. Only through his passion and death do we know that all human suffering is captured and transformed in and through his suffering. Only through his experience of darkness is all human evil and sin destroyed. Christ's defiance of death through the resurrection offers humanity hope that darkness does not have the last word, pain is not final, and sin can be overcome.

This ultimate act of redemption provides another view to human living: human beings can seek the supernatural and actually attain it. We do not grasp onto God who is Infinite but we can enter into an intimate relationship with the One True God and Divine Lover of all. Our pursuit of the supernatural that creates a continual angst within us is this desire for faith in a God who redeems and saves humanity from its own darkness and death. I contend that this is what most of the arts of popular culture seek to convey. Humanity desperately wants to make sense of human existence, and sometimes we find that only God can provide the answers. At times popular culture remains stubbornly anchored on the questions, unwilling or unable to make that leap of faith in a Loving God, One beyond our humanist perspective, who re-deems through suffering and death, such as in *Arrival, Life of Pi,* and the portrayal of Stephen Hawking in *The Theory of Everything.* At other times it stays with the darkness because it is conditioned through philosophical nihilism, which negates human and moral principles, to remove meaning from all of human existence and supernatural desires, such as in *Fight Club* when the narrator says, "I found freedom. Losing all hope was freedom."

Through the sacramental symbols and liturgical worship we touch the reality of supernatural grace in a material world. This thread of mystery and sacramentality provides a key to opening up the meaning of human hungers and angst revealed through popu-lar culture. They are the longings of human beings from every time and place. As God speaks through the prophet Jeremiah, he says, "More tortuous than all else is the human heart, beyond remedy; who can understand it?"[7] Yet, God continues, "I, the LORD, alone probe the mind and test the heart, to reward everyone according to his ways, according to the merit of his deeds."[8] When we touch upon what is authentically human, the whole person, we reach for the divine. The liturgy and sacraments provide a way of reading the culture's artifacts to discover grace present and the depths of meaning they seek to uncover and discover.

Becoming Cultural Mystics

If one can read in the many cultural symbols the elements of ✓ self-sacrifice, self-giving love and a search for truth, beauty, and goodness, or the struggle with existential darkness, then grace is present. These ideals are what give humanity hope. Despite the sinful tendencies of human beings to lie, kill, cheat, betray, and de-stroy, there is always a glimmer of hope in the soul that cannot be extinguished. It is that *supernatural existential* that burns in each human person leading them to desire union with the Divine, God,

7. Jer 17:9 (NABRE).
8. Jer 17:9–10 (NABRE).

who is Being Itself and Creator of all that is, and who communicates himself to humanity. Grace is God's self-communication. It is God's eternal love bestowed on humanity offering the possibility to live in the freedom of the children of God (Rom 8:21).

It takes cultural mystics who through a sacred look and attuned to grace indicate those very existential longings present in the popular culture. They are those who struggle with their own humanity and, so can speak to people's pains, struggles, and dreams unsanctimoniously. They are those who have been through the fire of doubt and have come out existentially free. They are those who see God's grace present in and through the cultural artifacts' symbols and signs and in humanity's hungering for *the more* than what this world can offer. These cultural mystics proclaim that it is God alone who can fill that void, and in the end, "he rewards those who seek him" (Heb 11:6).

Bibliography

Alberione, James. *Explanation of the Constitutions*. Translated by the Daughters of St. Paul USA. Boston: Daughters of St. Paul, 1961.

———. *Ut Perfectus Sit Homo Dei*. Translated by Mike Byrnes. Rome: Società di San Paolo, 1998.

Aquinas, Thomas. *The Summa Theologica of St. Thomas Aquinas*, Vol. I. Translated by the Fathers of the Dominican Province. New York: Christian Classics, 1981.

Augustine. *Confessions*. Translated by John K. Ryan. New York: Doubleday, 1960.

Benedict XVI, Pope. "Children and the Media: A Challenge for Education." Message of the Holy Father Benedict XVI for the 41st World Communications Day. Vatican, 2007.

———. *Credo for Today: What Christians Believe*. San Francisco: Ignatius, 2009.

———. *Spe Salvi: Encyclical Letter of Pope Benedict XVI on Saved in Hope*. Boston: Pauline Books & Media, 2007.

———. *The Transforming Power of Faith*. San Francisco: Ignatius, 2013.

Boyce, Frank Cottrell. "The Patron Saints of Cinema." *The Guardian*, October 20, 2004. https://www.theguardian.com/film/2004/oct/20/londonfilmfestival2004.londonfilmfestival.

Biskind, Peter. "An American Family." *Vanity Fair*, April 2007. http://www.vanityfair.com/news/2007/04/sopranos200704.

Blake, Richard A. *AfterImage: The Indelible Catholic Imagination of Six American Filmmakers*. Chicago: Loyola, 2000.

Catalano, Michael. "Where Have All the Rock Stars Gone?" *Forbes*, February 28, 2013. https://www.forbes.com/sites/michelecatalano/2013/02/28/where-have-all-the-rock-stars-gone/#668c659c2730.

Cessario, Romanus. "The Theological Virtue of Hope." In *The Ethics of Aquinas*, edited by Stephen Pope, 232–43. Washington, DC: Georgetown University Press, 2002.

Congregation of the Doctrine of the Faith. *Catechism of the Catholic Church.* Vatican: Libreria Editrice Vaticana, 1993.

―――. *The Participation of Catholics in Political Life.* Vatican, 2002.

de Lubac, Henri. *The Splendor of the Church.* San Francisco: Ignatius, 1986.

Detweiler, Craig, and Barry Taylor. *A Matrix of Meanings: Finding God in Pop Culture.* Grand Rapids: Baker Academic, 2003.

Drushel, Bruce, and Kathleen German, eds. *Ethics of Emerging Media.* New York: Continuum, 2011.

Dulles, Avery. "John Paul II and the Mystery of the Human Person." *America,* February 2, 2004. www.americamagazine.org/issue/469/article/john-paul-ii-and-mystery-human-person.

Durrwell, F. X. *In the Redeeming Christ.* Notre Dame, IN: Ave Maria, 2013.

Ebert, Roger. "'Millions' Writer Wins 'Lottery.'" RobertEbert.com, March 13, 2005. http://www.rogerebert.com/interviews/millions-writer-wins-lottery.

Egan, Harvey D. "The Mystical Theology of Karl Rahner." *The Way* 52 (April 2013). http://www.theway.org.uk/back/522egan.pdf.

Eggemeier, Matthew T. *A Sacramental-Prophetic Vision: Christian Spirituality in a Suffering World.* Collegeville, MN: Liturgical, 2014.

Eliade, Mircea. *Symbolism, the Sacred & the Arts.* Edited by Diane Apostolos-Cappadona. New York: Continuum, 1985.

Ess, Charles. *Digital Media Ethics.* Cambridge, UK: Polity, 2009.

Forte, Bruno. *The Portal of Beauty: Toward a Theology of Aesthetics.* Grand Rapids: Eerdmans, 2008.

Francis, Pope. Homily of His Holiness Pope Francis, "Easter Vigil in the Holy Night." Vatican Basilica, April 4, 2015.

―――. "Our Encounter with Jesus Fills Our Hearts with Joy." General Audience, August 4, 2013. http://www.news.va/en/news/pope-francis-our-encounter-with-jesus-fills-our-he.

Frith, Simon. *Performing Rites: On the Value of Popular Music.* Cambridge: Harvard University Press, 1996.

Garcia-Rivera, Alejandro R. *A Wounded Innocence: Sketches for a Theology of Art.* Collegeville, MN: Liturgical, 2003.

Gleeson, Brian. "Symbols and Sacraments: Their Human Foundations." *Australian eJournal of Theology* 2 (February 2004). http://aejt.com.au/__data/assets/pdf_file/0007/395674/AEJT_2.10_Gleeson_Symbols_and_Sacraments.pdf.

Godzieba, Anthony J. "The Catholic Sacramental Imagination and the Access/Excess of Grace." *New Theology Review* 21 (August 2008) 14–26.

Greeley, Andrew. *The Catholic Imagination.* Berkeley: University of California Press, 2000.

Grenz, Stanley J. *A Primer on Postmodernism.* Grand Rapids: Eerdmans, 1996.

Herbert, Geoff. "Sex Sells: 92 Percent of Top 10 Billboard Charts Are About Sex, Study Finds." *Syracuse.com,* October 4, 2011. http://blog.syracuse.com/entertainment/2011/10/billboard_top_10_songs_about_sex_suny_albany_study.html.

Holmes, Gary. "Can Television Be High Art?" *Mediapost.com,* March 5, 2013. https://www.mediapost.com/publications/article/194947/can-television-be-high-art.html.

John Paul II, Pope. *Ex Corde Ecclesiae.* Vatican: Libreria Editrice Vaticana, 1990. http://w2.vatican.va/content/john-paul-ii/en/apost_constitutions/documents/hf_jp-ii_apc_15081990_ex-corde-ecclesiae.html.

———. *Fides et Ratio: On the Relationship Between Faith and Reason.* Boston: Pauline Books, 1998.

———. *God, Father and Creator: A Catechesis on the Creed.* Boston: Pauline Books, 1996.

———. *Letter to Artists.* Vatican: Libreria Editrice Vaticana, 1999. https://w2.vatican.va/content/john-paul-ii/en/letters/1999/documents/hf_jp-ii_let_23041999_artists.html.

———. *Letter to Families from Pope John Paul II.* Boston: Pauline Books, 1994.

———. *Man and Woman He Created Them: A Theology of the Body.* Boston: Pauline Books, 2006.

———. "Sin Alienates the Human Person." General Audience, November 12, 1986. http://totus2us.com/teaching/jpii-catechesis-on-jesus-christ/sin-alienates-the-human-person.

———. *Veritatis Splendor.* Boston: Pauline Books, 1993.

Johnston, Robert. "Visual Christianity." In *The Conviction of Things Not Seen: Worship and Ministry in the 21st Century,* edited by Todd E. Johnson, 165–82. Grand Rapids: Brazos, 2002.

Jungel, Eberhard. *God as the Mystery of the World.* Grand Rapids: Eerdmans, 1983.

Kaczor, Christopher. *Thomas Aquinas on Faith, Hope, and Love: Edited and Explained for Everyone.* Ave Maria, FL: Sapientia, 2008.

Ladaria, Luis F. *Jesus Christ Salvation of All.* Miami: Convivium, 2008.

Larsen, Kari. "Those Who Reject the Art of Television Are Doomed." *Mic.com,* August 13, 2013. https://mic.com/articles/58381/those-who-reject-the-art-of-television-are-doomed#.UzgLTd3ra.

Lennan, Richard, and Nancy Pineada-Madrid, eds. *Hope: Promise, Possibility, and Fulfillment.* Mahwah, NJ: Paulist, 2013.

Marks, Richard. "Is Television Now the Predominant Art Form—Quite Literally?" *Research the Media,* March 15, 2013. https://researchthemedia.com/2013/03/15/is-television-now-the-predominant-art-form-quite-literally/.

McArdle, Patrick. "Ecce Homo: Theological Perspectives on Personhood and the Passions." *Australian eJournal of Theology* 7 (June 2006). http://aejt.com.au/__data/assets/pdf_file/0007/395737/AEJT_7.18_McArdle.pdf.

McBrien, Richard. *Catholicism.* Revised and updated edition. North Blackburn: Collins Dove, 1994.

McCracken, Brett. "Alejandro Gonzalez Iñárritu Talks to Christianity Today About 'The Revenant.'" *Christianity Today,* December 21, 2015. http://

www.christianitytoday.com/ct/2015/december-web-only/alejandro-gonzlez-irritu-talks-to-ct-about-revenant.html.

McGinn, Bernard, ed. *Essential Writings of Christian Mysticism.* New York: Random House, 2006.

Melas, Chloe. "Selena Gomez Opens Up About '13 Reasons Why' and Her Own Struggles." *CNN Entertainment,* March 28, 2017. http://www.cnn.com/2017/02/08/entertainment/selena-gomez-13-reasons-why/index.html.

Merton, Thomas. *The New Man.* New York: Farrar, Straus and Giroux, 1961.

Millbank, John, Catherine Pickstock, and Graham Ward, eds. *A Radical Orthodoxy: A New Theology.* New York: Routledge, 1999.

"Morality of 'The Departed.'" *Beliefnet.com.* http://www.beliefnet.com/Entertainment/Movies/2006/10/Morality-Of-The-Departed.aspx?p=3.

Nouwen, Henri. *Behold the Beauty of the Lord: Praying with Icons.* Notre Dame, IN: Ave Maria, 2007.

O'Collins, Gerald. *Christology: A Biblical, Historical, and Systematic Study of Jesus.* New York: Oxford University Press, 1995.

O'Donovan, Leo, ed. *A World of Grace: An Introduction to the Themes and Foundations of Karl Rahner's Theology.* Washington, DC: Georgetown University Press, 1995.

Pontifical Council for Justice and Peace. *Compendium of the Social Doctrine of the Church.* Vatican: Libreria Editrice Vaticana, 2004.

Pontifical Council for Social Communications. *Ethics in Communications.* Boston: Pauline Books, 2000.

Rahner, Karl. *The Content of Faith.* New York: Crossroad, 2000.

———. *Foundations of Christian Faith: An Introduction to the Idea of Christianity.* Translated by William V. Dych. New York: Crossroad, 1978.

———. "Jesus Christ—The Meaning of Life." In *Theological Investigations 21,* translated by Hugh Riley, 178–96. New York: Crossroad, 1988.

———. *Karl Rahner: Theologian of the Graced Search for Meaning.* Edited by Geffrey B. Kelly. Minneapolis: Fortress, 1992.

———. *The Mystical Way in Everyday Life.* Maryknoll, NY: Orbis 2011.

———. "On the Theology of Worship." In *Theological Investigations 19,* translated by Edward Quinn, n.p. New York: Crossroad, 1983.

———. *A Rahner Reader.* Edited by Gerald A. McCool. New York: Seabury, 1975.

———. "Theology of Freedom." In *Theological Investigations 6,* translated by Karl H. and Boniface Kruger, 141–49. Baltimore: Helicon, 1969.

Ratzinger, Josef. *Introduction to Christianity.* New York: Herder & Herder, 1970.

Remnick, David. "Family Guy: The End of 'The Sopranos.'" *The New Yorker,* June 4, 2007. http://www.newyorker.com/magazine/2007/06/04/family-guy.

Robinson, Tasha. "*Calvary's* Writer-Director and Star on Faith, Hope, and Glorified Suicide." *Thedissolve.com,* August 8, 2014. https://thedissolve.com/features/interview/697-calvarys-writer-director-and-star-on-faith-hope-an.

Rolnick, Philip A. *Person, Grace, and God*. Grand Rapids: Eerdmans, 2007.

Ross, Susan A. *Anthropology*. Collegeville, MN: Liturgical, 2012.

Roth, Veronica. *Divergent*. New York: Katherine Tegen, 2011. Kindle.

Sarachik, Justin. "Chance the Rapper Losing God Helped Him to Create Music as a 'Christian Man.'" *rapzilla.com,* May 26, 2016. http://www.rapzilla.com/rz/features/13483-chance-the-rapper-losing-god-helped-him-create-music-as-christian-man.

Scharer, Matthias, and Bernd Jochen Hilberath. *The Practice of Communicative Theology: An Introduction to a New Theological Culture*. New York: Crossroad, 2008.

Schonborn, Christoph. *Man, the Image of God: The Creation of Man as Good News*. San Francisco: Ignatius, 2011.

Shea, John. *Stories of God: An Unauthorized Biography*. Chicago: Thomas More, 1978.

Storey, John. *Cultural Studies and the Study of Popular Culture*. 2nd ed. Athens: University of Georgia Press, 2003.

Szostek, Andrzej. "Karol Wojtyla's View of the Human Person in the Light of the Experience of Morality." In vol. 60 of *Existential Personalism*, edited by Daniel O. Dahlstrom, 50–64. Washington, DC: American Catholic Philosophical Association, 1986.

Till, Rupert. *Pop Cult: Religion and Popular Music*. London: Continuum, 2010.

Tracy, David. *The Analogical Imagination: Christian Theology and the Culture of Pluralism*. New York: Crossroad, 1981.

Vatican Council II. *Gaudium et Spes; Pastoral Constitution of the Church in the Modern World Promulgated by Pope Paul IV*. Vatican, 1965.

Viladesau, Richard. *Theological Aesthetics: God in Imagination, Beauty and Art*. New York: Oxford University Press, 1999.

Von Balthasar, Hans Urs. *Engagement With God*. San Francisco: Ignatius, 2008.

———. *The Glory of the Lord: Theological Aesthetics, Volume 1: Seeing the Form*. Translated by Erasmo Leva-Merikakis. San Francisco: Ignatius, 1982.

———. *Love Alone is Credible*. San Francisco: Ignatius, 2004.

———. *The Von Balthasar Reader*. Edited by Medard Kehl and Werner Loser. New York: Crossroad, 1982.

White, Armond. "Film is Art, Television a Medium." *The New York Times,* April 3, 2014. https://www.nytimes.com/roomfordebate/2014/04/03/television-tests-tinseltown/film-is-art-television-is-a-medium.

Wojtyla, Karol. *The Acting Person*. Edited by Anna-Teresa Tymieniecka. Translated by Andrzej Potocki. Analecta Husserliana 10. Doredrecht, Holland: D. Reidel, 1979.

———. *Love and Responsibility*. San Francisco: Ignatius, 1993.

———. *Person and Community: Selected Essays*. Translated by Theresa Sandok. New York: Peter Lang, 1993.

———. *Toward a Philosophy of Praxis*. Edited by Alfred Bloch and George T. Czuczka. New York: Crossroad, 1980.

Index